THIS ENGLAND
ANNUAL 2023

Celebrate the best of England

Events • People • Places • Views

Welcome

to our *This England* Annual 2023, full of our usual mixed bag of treats to enjoy and dip into throughout the year.

As a country we really do have a wealth of inventive and quirky traditions and after the uncertainty of the last couple of years, it seems that people are embracing them more than ever, enjoying the communal experiences. Our guides offer many, from sausage festivals to coal-carrying championships.

We also have a great selection of longer read features, starting off with Leeds – which is doing Capital of Culture its own way in 2023. We visit Cornwall's spectacular gardens, mark the birth of the supermarket, revisit the scandal of Piltdown Man and look at the *Windrush* legacy, as well as exploring husky racing and visiting the British Library, and there's plenty more too. Enjoy!

Angela

Angela Linforth, Editor.

CONTENTS

26

50

98

90

94

Cover and opening spread: Trebah Gardens. Credits: Shutterstock, Alamy
Back cover: York Gate Garden, Leeds. Credit: Shutterstock

Spring
by Andrea Hazeldine

New flowers each day
Woken from their rest,
Tiny spring buds
Are surely the best.

Birds call the dawn,
Days are bright.
Evenings are longer
And gently fade to night.

Spring arrives and
Nature renews fast.
Birds chirp loudly,
Their chorus says, "At last".

A beech wood near Painswick, Gloucestershire, with a light dusting of snow

WINTER TO SPRING

Chinese New Year, pancake racing, the British Library at 50, the first trans-Atlantic flight and Leeds embraces a year of culture in 2023 >

WINTER TO SPRING

Katherine Sorrell marks the start of women on the floor of the Stock Exchange, explores midwinter traditions and skipping

JANUARY 2023

NEW YEAR'S DAY PARADE

The capital's annual parade kicks off the year in style. More than 10,000 participants from around the world include

London's Parade

cheer squads and marching bands, floats and inflatables, historic vehicles, dancers and groups from West End shows. It starts at noon at Piccadilly Circus and winds its way, via Pall Mall and Trafalgar Square, to a grand finish in Parliament Square. A mix of contemporary performances and traditional pomp and ceremony. **lnydp.com**

HAXEY HOOD

On 6 January each year, the village of Haxey takes part in a local tradition dating back to the 14th century. It's a kind of huge great rugby scrum or "sway" with no official teams and

A Haxey participant

very few rules; the aim being to manoeuvre the "hood" (which was once a bullock's head but now is a two-foot length of leather) towards one of the pubs. With around 200 people participating and 1,000 or so watching, the whole thing is presided over by a Lord, a Fool and 11 referees known as Boggins, who, in the week preceding, tour local pubs in festival costume and sing traditional folk songs. **wheewall.com/hood**

WHITTLESEA STRAW BEAR FESTIVAL

Bizarre and unique: a man wrapped in a coat of straw makes quite a sight in the town of Whittlesea, Cambridgeshire. It's the revival of an ancient tradition that's linked to Plough Monday (see right), though no one quite knows where it originated. These days there's a three-day festival (in 2023 from 13-15 January), with the finale on the Saturday involving more than 250 dancers, musicians and performers performing traditional "Molly", "Morris", "Clog" and "Sword" dancing. It all ends with a ceremonial burning of the costume on Sunday, leaving the way open for a new bear to be created from next season's harvest. **strawbear.org.uk**

BOLNEY APPLE HOWLING

The Chanctonbury Ring Morris Men lead the apple "howling" – another form of wassail – at Old Mill Farm, Bolney, Sussex, on the first Saturday in January. Popular with families, it starts with a torchlit procession and continues with an invitation to thrash the trunks of the apple trees with sticks, followed by the wassail song and dances by the Morris Men. It all ends with a "general hullabaloo" in which everyone makes as much noise as possible. Bring your own saucepan or football rattle. **crmm.org.uk/applehowling.html**

SNOWDROP FESTIVAL

It is always a delight to spot the first snowdrops delicately emerging from the ground – a sure sign that winter is coming to an end. Galanthophiles (that's snowdrop lovers to you and me) will not want to miss the Snowdrop Festival at The Garden House in Buckland Monachorum, Devon. Here, from mid-January until the end of February, visitors can enjoy more than 350 varieties in bloom around the gardens, and also buy their own bulbs from specialist nursery sales. **thegardenhouse.org.uk**

PLOUGH SUNDAY AND MONDAY

Plough Monday, the first Monday after Twelfth Night, was traditionally the start of the English agricultural year, with farm workers returning – perhaps reluctantly – to the fields. In some parts of the country it was common to drag a plough through their villages, collecting money while singing, dancing and performing

plays. The local church blessed the plough, either on the same day or on Plough Sunday. Durham has the oldest recorded mention of the ceremony in England, from 1413, when an official from Durham Priory presented four pence to the group drawing the plough. The custom died out in the 19th century, but has been revived in recent years, in Durham, Northwold in Norfolk, and elsewhere. Expect Morris dancing, parades, fancy dress, traditional music, church services and festive cheer. The Morris Ring has a list of Plough Sunday and Monday Morris events. **themorrisring.org**

SLAPSTICK FESTIVAL

Bristol's annual celebration of silent and visual comedy brings together an array of leading comedians, comedy writers, biographers, film historians, musicians and more in this UNESCO City of Film. From screenings of some of the best silent films ever made to stand-up sessions, talks and performances, it's a great antidote to long, dark winter nights. **slapstick.org.uk**

THE FLEECE INN WASSAIL

Wassailing is an ancient custom that involves singing to apple trees to wake them from their winter slumbers and scare away evil spirits. There is a growing number of wassailing events around the country. At the Fleece Inn, near Evesham in Worcestershire, for example, there's cider, singing, Morris dancers and hanging toast in the branches as a gift to the tree spirits. **thefleeceinn.co.uk**

HOLLY HOLY DAY

On 25 January, 1644 the siege of Nantwich was lifted by parliamentary forces. The Cheshire town holds an annual celebration called "Holly Holy Day" because locals wore sprigs of holly in their hats. As well as a battle re-enactment by the Sealed Knot society, there's a parade, live music, refreshments, morris dancing and a wreath-laying ceremony. **battleofnantwich.org**

Midwinter customs on the Thames

BANKSIDE TWELFTH NIGHT

Staged by professional performers The Lions part, Twelfth Night is an annual collective celebration of the new year held in the Bankside area of London. Starting with piping the Holly Man and Beelzebub over the Thames, and concluding with storytelling, dancing and mulled wine in the ancient George Inn in Southwark, it combines ancient midwinter customs with contemporary festivities. **thelionspart.co.uk/ twelfthnight**

CHINESE NEW YEAR, LONDON

The Chinese Year of the Rabbit begins on 22 January 2023, and celebrations will take place in major cities around the UK, including London, Manchester, Liverpool, Birmingham, Leeds, Southampton and elsewhere. The capital's Chinese New Year celebrations are the biggest outside Asia, and involve hundreds of thousands of people descending on the West End for a host of spectacular free events, including a huge parade, lion dances and a variety of stage performances. **visitlondon.com**

90 YEARS YOUNG

The world's first underground railway opened in London in 1863. Various maps were developed, but, though originally considered too radical, a trial print run in January 1933 proved Harry Beck's diagrammatic map was just what the public wanted.

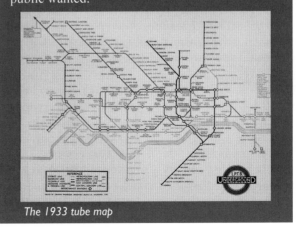

The 1933 tube map

The Nobel Prize is presented to Francis Crick

DNA STRUCTURE DISCOVERED 70 YEARS AGO

On 28 February 1953, Cambridge University scientists James Watson and Francis Crick, aided by Rosalind Franklin, determined the structure of DNA – and announced it in the nearby Eagle pub, saying: "We have found the secret of life". Their discovery solved the mystery of how genetic instructions are passed between generations and revolutionised the study of biology and medicine, leading to such game-changing developments as pre-natal screening for genetic diseases and the accurate testing of criminal evidence.

HURLING THE SILVER BALL

The St Ives Feast Day, on the first Monday after 3 February, starts with a civic procession for the blessing at the St Ia's Well near Porthmeor Beach, followed by one of Cornwall's most ancient customs: the "hurling" of a silver ball. In this boisterous game, a form of rugby, participants attempt to win the cricket ball-sized ball from each other around the town (and sometimes in the sea). It's several hours of rough and tumble, and the group often travels a few miles and back, with one aim: whoever returns the ball to the mayor on the steps of St Ives Guildhall on the stroke of midday receives a silver coin. In the afternoon, pennies are proffered from the balcony by town councillors to waiting children on the Guildhall forecourt. **stivestowncouncil-cornwall.gov.uk/news-and-events/st-ives-feast-day**

KESWICK FILM FESTIVAL

This friendly film festival – known as Cumbria's answer to Sundance – is usually held in February or March and offers a programme of the best of world and independent cinema, with everything from blockbusters to documentaries, plus previews, classics, retrospectives, shorts, talks and special guests. **keswickfilm.org/festival**

PANCAKE RACING

The world-famous event in Olney, Buckinghamshire, is said to have first been run in 1445 and always takes place on Shrove Tuesday. The race of 415 yards is open to 25 female residents of the town, who must wear an apron and headscarf and, of course, carry a frying pan and pancake. **olneypancakerace.org**

LENTSHERD

Every Shrove Tuesday, the aim of this intriguing custom in Clovelly, Devon, is to banish the devil into the sea before the start of Lent. To this end, local children drag tin cans down the village's steep cobbled street at dusk, making a deafening racket. At the harbour, the cans are tied together and thrown into the water (later to be retrieved and recycled!), taking the evil spirits with them. **clovelly.co.uk**

GRIMALDI CLOWN SERVICE

Joseph Grimaldi is known as the king of clowns, and scores of professional clowns of all descriptions, in full costume, pack the pews for this popular annual service (on the first Sunday in February) at All Saints Church in Haggerston, London. Arrive early for the service that includes hymns, readings, songs and performances. **clownsinternational.com**

CANDLEMAS

The Christian festival of Candlemas, which commemorates the presentation of Christ at the Temple, takes place on 2 February each year. At Yorkshire's Ripon Cathedral, more than 7,000 candles are arranged in beautiful displays, illuminating its architectural glories for a service attended by hundreds of people. **riponcathedral.org.uk**

JORVIK VIKING FESTIVAL

Taking place at the same time of year (in modern times, half-term week), this annual family-friendly festival, the largest of its kind in Europe, celebrates the city of York's heritage of almost a century of Viking rule. Look out for the living history encampment, strongest Viking competition and best beard contest, as well as battles, marches and banquets. **jorvikvikingfestival.co.uk**

"MOB" FOOTBALL

These violent contests between two villages, often on public holidays, were so unruly they became the subject of royal bans. Survivors include the Royal Shrovetide Football Match at Ashbourne, Derbyshire, a huge event on Shrove Tuesday and Ash Wednesday; Shrove Tuesday Football at Alnwick Castle; and Atherstone Football, Warwickshire, where the winner is the one holding the ball at the end of the match.

SKIPPING DAY

For well over a century, Shrove Tuesday in Scarborough has been a day not just for pancake racing but also traditional long-rope skipping on the beachfront. It begins at noon, and hundreds usually take part, with most local children given the afternoon off school. **scarboroughsmaritime heritage.org.uk**

IMAGINE CHILDREN'S FESTIVAL

An arts festival like no other, Imagine Children's Festival is dedicated to families experiencing and enjoying all kinds of art and culture together. Liven up a half-term week with a visit to the Southbank Centre, London, for the best theatre, music, literature, comedy, dance and wellbeing, more than half of it completely free. **southbankcentre.co.uk**

RHUBARB FESTIVAL

From crumble to gin, most of the rhubarb we consume in the UK is grown in Yorkshire's "rhubarb triangle". One of the first food and drink festivals of the year, the annual rhubarb extravaganza at Wakefield features chef demos, a food and drink market, gardening workshops, arts and crafts stalls, comedy, live music and all sorts of family fun. **experiencewakefield. co.uk**

DARK SKIES FESTIVALS

Our star-studded skies are celebrated at winter festivals in the North York Moors, Yorkshire Dales, Cumbria, Northumberland, Exmoor and the South Downs. Previous activities include UV rockpooling, night-time canoeing, art workshops, forest walks, expert talks and, of course, stargazing. **darkskiesnationalparks.org.uk**

100 YEARS SINCE THE UNSEALING OF THE TOMB OF TUTANKHAMUN

English archaeologist Howard Carter uncovered the entrance in 1922. After months of cataloguing objects from the outer tomb, he reached the burial chamber, and on 16 February 1923 he found the best-preserved royal tomb ever discovered. A beautiful chamber contained an enormous shrine surrounding a stone sarcophagus and three coffins, the innermost made of solid gold.

70 YEARS AGO: THE END OF SWEET RATIONING

On 5 February 1953 the rationing of sweets came to an end. For 11 years everyone over five years old had been limited to seven ounces of sweets per day – and even this small amount was not always available. Piggy banks were emptied and hordes of children raced to the shops. The BBC reported toffee apples were the biggest seller, with strips of nougat and liquorice strips also selling fast.

The untold joy of a sweet shop

The Stock Exchange in the 1970s

50TH ANNIVERSARY OF WOMEN IN THE STOCK EXCHANGE

After decades of campaigning, on 26 March 1973 six newly elected female stockbrokers set foot on the floor of "the house", the first time any women, other than the Queen, had been admitted into the London Stock Exchange in its almost 200-year history. That seems shocking now!

FIVE DECADES OF THE MODERN LONDON BRIDGE

Ancient London grew around London Bridge, the only bridge across the Thames for centuries. After a succession of timber bridges, a medieval stone construction stood for 622 years, until it was replaced in 1831 by a new stone-arched version. As 20th-century traffic built up, however, the "new" bridge began to sink into the Thames, and the decision was taken to replace it (sold at auction, it was pulled down piece by piece and rebuilt in Arizona by an American developer). The current London Bridge – designed by William Holford and made from concrete and steel – was opened by the Queen on 17 March 1973.

The old London Bridge, circa 1900

THE BOAT RACE

One of the world's oldest and most famous amateur sporting events, the annual rowing contest between crews from Oxford and Cambridge universities takes place close to Easter each year on the River Thames (this year scheduled for late March), along the 4.25 miles between Putney and Mortlake. There are places to watch the race for free along the full length of the course, with some of the best viewpoints being Putney Embankment near the start, Chiswick Pier in the centre and, for the final stages of the race, Dukes Meadow, a large park between Chiswick Bridge and Barnes Bridge. In 2022 Oxford won the men's race and Cambridge the women's race. **theboatrace.org**

Cambridge with a win

UK WIFE CARRYING RACE

Possibly related (though probably not) to the Viking raids of 12 centuries ago, this extraordinary event is run over a "very tough" 380m course at Dorking in Surrey. Rules are that males or females carry a "wife", who must be alive, human and at least 18 years old. They can be male or female, and do not need to be the carrier's actual wife. There's a minimum weight, and recognised holds include bridal, piggy-back, shoulder-ride, fireman's, Estonian and Dorking, or reverse Estonian. The prize? A national title, a barrel of local ale and £250 towards competing in the Finnish Wife Carrying Championships. **trionium.com/wife**

ST PIRAN'S DAY

On 5 March, the national day of Cornwall, a range of festivities are held around the county, from parades and concerts to mass singing of the Cornish anthem, *Trelawny*. Meanwhile, at the Eden Project, usually on the Saturday before St Piran's Day, don't miss the World Pasty Championships, with live music, comedy and the chance to enter your own Cornish pasty for an award. **cornishpastyassociation.co.uk**

THE CHELTENHAM FESTIVAL

The Cheltenham Festival is renowned for its boisterous atmosphere, in particular the roar from the stands at the start of the first race. It encompasses live music, shopping, world-class food and drink, and attracts some of the world's finest horses, with royalty and celebrities often in attendance. With 28 races over four days, each with its own headline event – and prize money averaging more than £1m per day – it culminates in Gold Cup Day and the prestigious steeplechase, run over three miles and two furlongs. **thejockeyclub.co.uk**

A porter at Aldermaston Station prior to closure

60TH BIRTHDAY OF THE BEECHING REPORT

It was one of the most notorious government reports of the 20th century. The "Beeching Report", actually named The Reshaping of British Railways, was issued on 27 March 1963 and proposed wholesale cuts to the national network. Dr Richard Beeching, its much-maligned author, was chairman of the British Railways Board, and his axe-wielding, still bitterly remembered today by many, resulted in the closure of both thousands of stations and thousands of miles worth of railways.

ORANGES AND LEMONS SERVICE

In medieval times, the churchyard of St Clement Danes in Westminster reached the bank of the Thames, and cargoes of fruit were brought through it. Since 1919, when a service was organised to mark the rehanging of the bells, the church has hosted an Oranges and Lemons Service, when children from the local primary school perform, each receiving an orange and a lemon to take home. **stclementdanesraf.org**

TICHBORNE DOLE

On Lady Day, 25 March, locals queue up to claim a gallon of flour each from outside Tichborne House in Hampshire. It is said to have begun in the late 12th century when Lady Tichborne lay dying and Sir Roger consented to provide corn for the needy from as much land as his wife could travel around holding a lighted torch. She managed to crawl around 23 acres before it went out, and prophesied that the House of Tichborne would fall if the charity were discontinued.

CRUFTS

Established by Charles Cruft in 1891, this famous event held at the NEC in Birmingham boasts 20,000 entrants and is an essential date in any dog lover's calendar. Enjoy the shows, the flyball and heelwork to music, Scruffts (for crossbreeds), the Hero Dog Award and Discover Dogs, where visitors can meet breeds and find a match for their lifestyle. **crufts.org.uk**

Woof!

WOW LONDON

To mark International Women's Day on 8 March, speakers, musicians, comedians, artists, and activists come to the Southbank Centre for WOW – Women of the World, the London edition of the festival celebrating women, girls and non-binary people. WOW is a global movement that believes a gender-equal world is needed, possible and desirable, and it's just as welcoming to men and boys. **thewowfoundation.com**

DISCOVER LINCOLNSHIRE WEEKEND

Every March sees a weekend of free entry to attractions in and around Lincoln, as well as other free activities, special offers and a tempting street food festival. Highlights include rides on Lincoln's open-top tour bus, entry to Lincoln Cathedral, an open day at Lincoln Guildhall and guided tours of the city. **visitlincoln.com**

WORDS BY THE WATER

From William Wordsworth to Beatrix Potter, many writers have been inspired by the Lake District. Words by the Water is a literature festival at Theatre by the Lake, Keswick. Sharing the pleasure of words and ideas over 10 days, the event brings over 100 writers and thousands of festival-goers together. **wayswithwords.co.uk**

Images: Shutterstock and Alamy

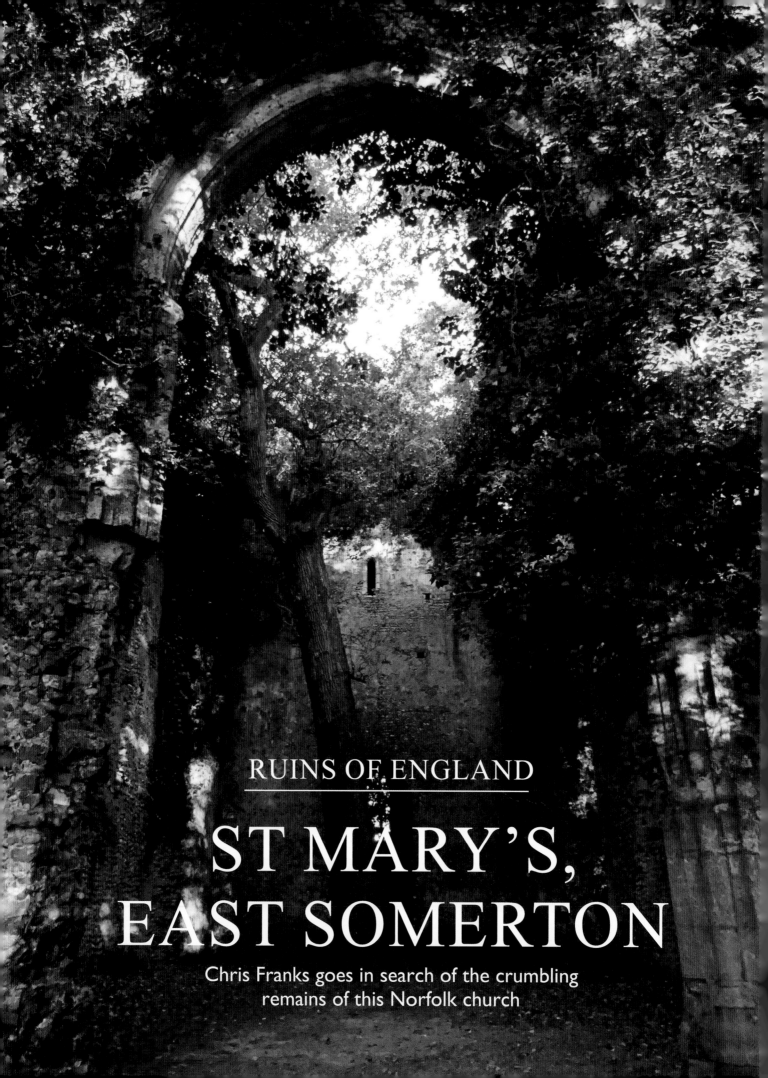

RUINS OF ENGLAND

ST MARY'S, EAST SOMERTON

Chris Franks goes in search of the crumbling
remains of this Norfolk church

The ruin is covered in ivy

IT'S early. A shadowy lilac still lurks on the horizon. The narrow back lane I've come on has led to a tunnel through a dense copse. As I get out of the car, a gust tugs at the leaves and a loud hiss swells, like an army of snakes. I look around. So where is it?

I've come to find the ruin of St Mary's Church, East Somerton, in Norfolk. When I first saw the pictures of crumbling fragments in a wood, something made me want to visit, some curious sense of urgency to see it before it was gone forever.

A narrow track disappears into the foliage. As I part the branches, a black mass begins to emerge, several metres high, its upper reaches smothered with tangles of ivy. In the nave walls are two holes, once windows but now opened to the ground, as if someone has driven a bulldozer through them. At one end are the remains of a tower, narrow as a lift shaft, with vines cascading down inside. At the other end is a chancel arch, the stone still a fresh sandy yellow.

I'm surrounded by jungle, yet inside, the ground is bare – except for the thing for which this ruin is famous. A huge oak tree with a two-foot-thick trunk is growing in the middle of the nave. There is a legend that a witch with a wooden leg was buried alive here and when the church was built over the grave, the oak tree grew from her leg, destroying the building. In the surreal pre-dawn gloom, I can almost believe it.

It looks incongruous to have a church built around a tree, but then I remember that it was the church that came first. This place has been deserted for nearly 350 years. Almost nothing is known about it. The oldest part is the tower, dating from the 13th century with two of its original three storeys still standing. The nave is 15th century and although the chancel arch is the best-preserved feature, nothing of the chancel itself remains.

Located in the grounds of Burnley Hall, St Mary's Church was originally a separate parish before being absorbed into another nearby. Toward the end of its life, it served as a chapel of ease for the Hall's residents. It was abandoned sometime in the latter 17th century, though by then, the chancel may have already been in ruin. It is now Grade II listed.

As I pace around, I long to see it in its heyday; the soaring tower, the rainbow stained glass, the bells tolling and people congregating. And yet, if it had been intact, I would never have bothered coming. Why do we appreciate things only once they are lost?

The sun rises. Fragments of gold trickle through the canopy, igniting the stones. I follow the track back to the road. There's another gust of wind and the leaves hiss again. I turn back for a final look. It has vanished.

Images: Chris Franks

LIVELY LEEDS

Sarah Freeman on how this Yorkshire city is
doing Capital of Culture its own way in 2023

IT was late morning on 23 November 2017 when the bombshell was dropped. Leeds had submitted its bid to become European Capital of Culture in 2023 and was quietly confident of success. It had every reason to be. A few years earlier, the city had proved it could host a world-class event by successfully staging the opening leg of the Tour de France. That, coupled with its already rich cultural history – it is the only city outside London to have permanent opera, theatre, ballet and contemporary dance companies – meant Leeds was one of the favourites to land the prestigious European title.

However, the ink was barely dry on its ambitious plans when it was announced that the UK would no longer be eligible to host the event. The European Commission cited Brexit, and while the government scrambled to save the event, ministers were met with a proverbial brick wall. It wasn't just Leeds, which had already invested £1m in its bid, that missed out. Dundee, Nottingham, Milton Keynes and Belfast/Derry also saw their hopes dashed.

However, as the new year dawned it was Leeds, channelling some of the famous Yorkshire grit for which it is known, that publicly shook off its disappointment. When it announced it was going ahead with a year-long programme of cultural events, some thought it foolhardy. Without the pot of European cash which comes with Capital of Culture status, there were fears the end result might be a poor shadow of the city's original plans, resulting in an anti-climax rather than a statement of intent.

However, the city has a long history of doing things its own way and the Leeds 2023 bandwagon didn't just roll, it quickly gathered momentum. Fast-forward to today, and thanks to a £35m investment from both the public and private sectors, Leeds is shaping up to host one big 12-month party under the banner, "Letting Culture Loose".

"Of course it was disappointing when the rug was pulled from under the bid," Abigail Scott Paul, from Leeds 2023, said. "However, it has also allowed us to throw out the rulebook. The year-long festival we are now designing is completely our own, there are absolutely no boxes which we have to tick."

Leeds's past is writ large in the city's architecture. Its grand public buildings date back to the Victorian Age when Leeds emerged as a textile powerhouse. Today finance and legal firms have taken the place of mills and factories and while its historic landmarks will provide the backdrop to events during its year of culture, the aim is to showcase the stories of those living there today.

"We are really proud that there are 170 languages spoken here and that as a city we are home to so many diverse communities," Abigail said. "Hidden among the sandstone and red brick buildings are millions of unseen stories about the people who made Leeds and those who are writing new chapters every day."

Top of Leeds's claims to fame is arguably the fact that it is home to the oldest West Indian carnival in Western Europe, which every August bank holiday turns the city into a riot of colour. It is also the base for a leading contemporary dance company. Phoenix Dance Theatre was founded in the 1980s by a group of black dancers who have continued to nurture talent from the streets they grew up in. Elsewhere, South Asian Arts-uk has been bringing South Asian classical music and dance to audiences across the city for nearly 25 years.

However, Leeds has often shied away from spotlighting its cultural successes – if 2023 achieves what it hopes to, this should be the start of a more confident era.

"Leeds Art Gallery and the

Inder Goldfinger and David Hamilton "letting culture loose"

Opera North at Leeds Grand Theatre

Leeds's famous West Indian Carnival

Henry Moore Institute are rightly lauded for their collections of British sculpture," Abigail said. "Opera North, Leeds Playhouse and Northern Ballet have all become renowned for staging ground-breaking productions, with historic venues like Leeds Grand Theatre and the City Varieties rubbing shoulders with the

>

The much-loved Kirkgate Market

> Brudenell Social Club, which in recent years has become a favourite with bands on the touring circuit. Leeds has a real cultural depth."

However, Leeds 2023 wants to recognise that culture means different things to different people and attract the widest audience possible. This may go some way in explaining why instead of asking Ricky Wilson, frontman of Leeds band Kaiser Chiefs, to be the face of the Leeds 2023 promotional video, organisers instead went with Parkour World Champion David Nelmes, who honed his skills on the city's streets.

"Culture doesn't just mean theatre or film or painting and we want Leeds 2023 to reflect that," Abigail said. "Yes, this will be a celebration of traditional arts, but it will also be a celebration of the city's food scene, its sporting stars and its best creative minds, whatever sector they happen to work in."

Pinning their colours to the mast, one of the cornerstones of Leeds 2023 is the Smeaton 300 Project, which aims to create a lasting tribute to the work of pioneer John Smeaton and the city's civil engineering legacy. Born in Leeds in 1724, Smeaton was a self-taught engineer, inventor and

collaborator. He designed lighthouses, bridges, piers and canals, but unlike Isambard Kingdom Brunel, his name is largely unknown outside of engineering circles.

"He was an engineer who described himself as an artist and that completely dovetails with our ambitions to be as inclusive as possible," Abigail added. "Culture can sometimes feel niche or exclusive, but everything we do in 2023 will be the exact opposite of that."

The full programme for Leeds 2023 will be announced in autumn 2022, 100 days before the official launch. However, what we do already know is that there will be 12 key events – one for each month of the year – and that they will act as springboards for cultural activities happening across the city.

Keen to prove the event will leave a lasting legacy for Leeds, organisers have also given their backing to the opening of a National Poetry Centre. The centre is the brainchild of Simon Armitage, whose decade-long tenure as Poet Laureate began in 2019, and the hope is that it will turn Leeds into the country's poetry heartland. "Leeds is an ideal location – accessible,

WHERE TO STAY

Dakota

This hotel chain takes its name from the airliner which made its maiden flight from New York to Chicago in 1936. Dakota became a byword for elegant but affordable air travel, and the people behind this brand have taken the same philosophy into the hospitality sector. Right in the heart of Leeds, Dakota is perfectly located for exploring Leeds's cultural offering.
8 Russell Street, Leeds LS1 5RN. 0113 322 6261; dakotahotels.co.uk

Quebecs Hotel

Grade II listed, this is the only independently owned luxury hotel in the city centre and hosts the likes of Coldplay among its regular guests. Built in 1891 as the Leeds County Liberal club, the distinctive terracotta brickwork means the hotel is a landmark in its own right. The Gallery Lounge, where you can admire the hotel's magnificent stained glass windows, is the perfect destination for afternoon tea.
9 Quebec Street, Leeds LS1 2HA. 0113 244 8989; quebecshotel.co.uk

The Bells

For something a little different try The Bells, a collection of five-star serviced apartments in an impressive Victorian building close to Leeds Minster and the famous Kirkgate Market. Derelict for 20 years before a major renovation project completed in 2017, each apartment comes with generous living areas, state-of-the-art kitchens, and super-king-size bedrooms. A 10-minute walk from the railway station, its main selling point is the hot tubs in each room from which guests can enjoy impressive views.
6 Church Row, Leeds LS2 7HD. 0113 344 9525; thebellsleeds.com

central, dynamic, contemporary, future-minded, people-oriented and community-aware," said Armitage, who was born and lives just a few miles away from Leeds. "The centre will offer a place that poets can call home – where you can borrow or buy books, perform readings, showcase work, write, eat, drink, debate and run workshops."

It is hoped the centre will take shape in the next few years, but before it opens its doors Leeds will gain another landmark which will acknowledge one of the city's more difficult chapters, thanks to Leeds 2023. Turner Prize nominee Yinka Shonibare has been commissioned to create a sculpture to commemorate British Nigerian Leeds resident David Oluwale, who drowned in the city's River Aire in 1969. His death followed years of mental ill health, and throughout his short life he suffered homelessness, racism and police persecution.

Shonibare has said he hopes the sculpture will serve as a "hopeful" memorial to Oluwale and a reminder of the dark days to which we must not return.

"It's a fitting legacy to an ordinary man, who will no doubt leave an extraordinary legacy," he said. "We have to honour him in this small way and hopefully, if people can learn about history, and the mistakes of history, they won't repeat them."

Shonibare's sculpture also represents something fundamental about Leeds 2023. The team want to turn the city into one giant playground where people can stumble across works of art and a variety of different things to do.

"During the pandemic when cultural organisations were shuttered, I think we all realised how much we need and value them," Abigail said. "Next year is about creating playful adventures that utilise parks and public spaces to bring communities and families together.

"We will commission original work which aims to bring together collaborators in new and different ways, enable original work from world-class artists and build international collaborations. It will be a celebration of Leeds, of its people and one to which everyone is welcome."
For all the latest news and details about the Leeds 2023 events programme go to leeds2023.co.uk.

GETTING AROUND

Leeds has excellent road and rail links. Lying at the end of the M1 and also on the M62, it is easily accessible by car, although parking in the city centre can be pricey.

The best option is to arrive by train. There are direct connections to London, Birmingham and Manchester. National Express also offers regular connections to all the country's major towns and cities. Leeds is easy to navigate on foot, but it is worth hopping on one of the water taxis which take visitors to and from Leeds Dock and Granary Wharf area.

The Playhouse is a key cultural venue in Leeds

READ ALL ABOUT IT

The British Library turns 50 in 2023, but its impressive collections date back hundreds of years, says Deborah Stone

WHEN you walk through the doors of the British Library into the light-filled foyer, there's a flight of steps up to a massive six-storey glass and bronze tower that dominates the modern building. It's lit from the inside and almost looks like an art installation but is, in fact, the distillation of centuries of knowledge – because inside the King's Library Tower is George III's incredible collection of priceless antique books.

This impressive sight is a reminder that although the British Library celebrates its 50th anniversary in 2023, its collections span thousands of years and tell

HM Queen Elizabeth at the library

stories from all over the world. There are at least 170 million items to view at the British Library, the largest public building built in Britain in the 20th century and one of London's busiest.

In 2019, before COVID restrictions, there were 1,364,700 visitors and while thousands of students and business people use the 12 Reading Rooms (for which you need a reader's card), well over half of visitors are drawn by the superb exhibitions, for talks and lectures, or just to use the café and its free WiFi.

The Euston Road site near St Pancras railway station also has a large sunny courtyard with a café and lots of public seating around Eduardo Paolozzi's bronze statue

BOSTON SPA REPOSITORY

If you're wondering how the British Library manages to store 170 million items at its site next to St Pancras station, the answer is that it doesn't. Three quarters are kept at Boston Spa repository near Wetherby, West Yorkshire.

Boston Spa was home to the National Lending Library for Science and Technology when it was incorporated into the British Library in 1973. Then in 2013, 535 articulated lorries spent six months transporting Colindale Newspaper Library's millions of newspapers, magazines and journals to Boston Spa's state-of-the-art airtight storage. Thanks to the Legal Deposit Act the 44-acre campus – on the site of a former World War II munitions factory – also provides a home for every book or printed item published or distributed in Britain that is not being kept in London, which is most of them.

"The collection grows constantly, requiring 8km of new shelving every year – roughly the length of 80 football pitches," says a spokesperson.

Visitors to Boston Spa reading room have access to 85 per cent of the content available at St Pancras once they have been approved for a free reader's pass. A £95m project to increase storage facilities here will include a new reading room, restaurant and café plus viewing gallery in a new fully automated building.

Part of the government's "levelling up" policy but also a vital response to the never-ending need for more space, this will transform accessibility to British Library collections in the North when it's completed in 2026.

of Sir Isaac Newton, hunched over his scientific papers.

For this is no ordinary reference library: while the Reading Rooms are suitably hushed and studious the rest of the building is full of a sort of buzzing excitement. After all, it's not every day you can see an original version of the 1215 Magna Carta written on sheepskin parchment – you can buy a copy in the excellent gift shop for £25.

Without having to book tickets or pay an entrance fee, you can also see two original editions of Chaucer's *Canterbury Tales*, probably printed in 1476 and 1483; the first collected edition of William Shakespeare's plays, published in 1623; the Lindisfarne Gospels – written and illustrated by monks in the first century; two of only 48 surviving Gutenberg 1455 Bibles; and Handel's handwritten *Messiah*.

These are all in free exhibition rooms such as the permanent Treasures of The British Library, where you can also read John Lennon's original handwritten lyrics for The Beatles' songs *Strawberry Fields Forever*, *She Said She Said* and *In My Life*.

State-of-the-art storage facilities and display cabinets mean that light, temperature, humidity and pollution are constantly monitored to keep the collections safe and there are teams of conservators who specialise in the treatments required for everything from paper to parchment and vellum and from photographs to textiles.

It's a far cry from conditions in 1753, when the extensive collections of physician and naturalist Sir Hans Sloane were purchased for the nation for £20,000. This became the basis of the British Museum in 1759, the world's oldest national public museum, with the British Museum Library created within it.

Rare volumes from the Royal Library of King George II were among collections bequeathed to the nation that made their way to the museum's library. These also included the Cotton Library, with antiquarian documents such as the *Beowulf* manuscript, and King George III's enormous wide-ranging collection.

Eventually the museum's glorious domed Reading Room was built to house all the books in one place, opening in 1857 and attracting famous visitors down the years such as Charles Darwin, Charles Dickens, Virginia Woolf and George Bernard Shaw.

Even Karl Marx and Lenin have used the books kept here, with Lenin applying for a reader ticket under the pseudonym Jacob Richter. In 1907 he described it as "a remarkable institution, especially that exceptional reference section."

By the 1960s there were several libraries of national importance, so the 1972 British Library Act combined the National Lending Library for Science and Technology, The British National

The exterior of the building next to St Pancras Station

The sculpture of Newton in the courtyard

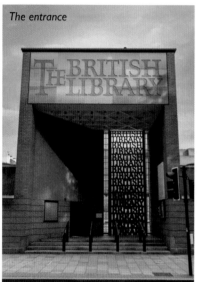

The entrance

> Bibliography, The British Museum Newspaper Library and The Patent Office Library into the British Library. The India Office Library and Records and the National Sound Archive were added in 1982 and 1983.

However, finding a site for the new British Library was financially and politically problematic. Plans to demolish streets in front of the British Museum for a new building were defeated. Then in 1976 the government bought the redundant Somers Town Goods Yard near St Pancras railway station for the new library. Building massive book storage basements was complicated by the nearby underground tube tunnels but the foundation stone was laid in 1982 and the building was expected to be completed in 1989.

Progress was snail-like and in 1995 *The Independent* newspaper suggested the library would cost "almost three times more than original official estimates" at more than £500 million.

It wasn't until 1997 that books and documents were finally transferred to the new building, which opened its doors to the public in November 1997 and was officially opened by the Queen in June 1998. Since then, despite criticism of its architectural design (notably from Prince Charles) it has been granted Grade I listed status and has become one of London's busiest public buildings.

Anybody can use the British Library and you can apply online for a free reader's pass at the library's website, bl.uk, although applicants must have a legitimate research reason for using it that can't be met elsewhere.

Once approved you can book an appointment to view items but these must be pre-ordered. It can take up to 48 hours for delivery from the 170 million books, journals, manuscripts, maps, stamps, music, patents, photographs, newspapers, sound recordings – even floppy discs, UK domain websites and blogs.

However, the online collection is growing – already up to four million digitised items from family history sources to Leonardo da Vinci's notebooks – and you can visit these free online from anywhere in the world, any time.

"Our public spaces are a place to research, to meet friends, to start up a new business or simply to get inspired by visiting our galleries and events," says a spokesperson. "We work with partners and libraries across the UK and the world to make sure that as many people as possible have the chance to use and explore our collections, events and expertise. And we're always open online, along with more and more of our digitised collection."

And that's not the end of the British Library story. Work to extend its Boston Spa repository is already underway while the government has committed £25m for a new public-access British Library in the North, at Temple Works – a Grade I listed former

flax mill in Leeds. Built in 1836, the building has a distinctive Egyptian temple façade and it's currently on Historic England's Heritage at Risk register. Not only will the new British Library project save the building but it will give even more people access to probably the world's greatest collection of documents and books. And hopefully, even Prince Charles will love the architecture.

BROUGHT TO BOOK

How well do you know your books? Nick Dalton puts you to the test

1. Which book set in Middle Earth was published in September 1937?

2. *On The Road*, published in September 1957, chronicled the travels of its author. Who was he?

3. David Tennant recently starred in a TV series of Jules Verne's *Around The World In 80 Days*. When was the first cinema version?
  A. 1952
  B. 1956
  C. 1960

4. Kenneth Branagh is Hercule Poirot in his new movie version of Agatha Christie's *Death on the Nile*, but who has played the Belgian detective most often?

5. "It was a bright cold day in April, and the clocks were striking thirteen" is the opening line of which 20th-century English novel?

6. *Harry Potter and the Philosopher's Stone* saw the young wizard's debut in 1997. How many copies has the book sold?
  A. 60 million
  B. 90 million
  C. 120 million

7. Which Yorkshire town celebrated the 125th anniversary of *Dracula* in 2022, and why?

8. Mark Billingham's 19th crime thriller, *The Murder Book*, starring Inspector Tom Thorne, was published in 2022. Where are the stories set?

9. In Jane Austen's *Emma*, who was Emma's love interest?

Q4

Q6

Q14

Q20

10. Which cheeky schoolboy favourite first appeared in 1922?

11. What was the first debut novel to be a Christmas No 1 bestseller? Clue: it was fairly recently.

12. How many romance novels does Mills & Boon publish each year?
  A. 200
  B. 400
  C. 700

13. "The Answer to the ultimate question of Life, the Universe and Everything is . . . 42!" is from which novel?

14. Kingsley Amis is the creator of which comic university lecturer?

15. "Literature is a luxury; fiction is a necessity" are the words of which author?

16. Which play features the stage direction "Exit, pursued by a bear"?

17. Whose 1919 novel *The Moon And Sixpence* was inspired by the life of artist Paul Gauguin?

18. *If I Don't Write It, Nobody Else Will* is the autobiography of a famed comedian – but who?

19. Horror author Stephen King has had more than 60 novels published but which was the first?

20. When did Winnie-the-Pooh first appear?

Answers on p107

Windsor Great Park and Windsor Castle

THE PUBLIC-PRIVATE REALM

Eleanor Doughty on the country's best privately owned public parks

THERE are few more wonderful activities than a leisurely walk in a beautiful place, with nature all around. Better still is the opportunity to walk in a place looked after by trusted gamekeepers, with its hedges trimmed, its lawn mowed – either by sheep or machine – and somewhere in the distance, an extraordinary piece of architecture punctuating the skyline.

As a resident of Windsor, Berkshire, this is a joy I am lucky enough to experience daily in Windsor Great Park, a huge portion of which is free for the public to explore, either on foot or by bicycle, and with dogs, too. With a healthy herd of red deer, it promises a delightful view of Windsor Castle from almost any angle.

Luckily, Windsor is not the only privately owned, publicly open park in England. Many of the others across the country are also attached to stately homes, having been designed to wow visitors with the work of landscape architects and make proud their owners, with avenues, rides, and glorious vistas spotted with follies.

Best of all, some of them – like Windsor – offer free public access, provided you stick to their gentle rules. These parks are priceless, with their unspoiled scenery. Privately owned, they haven't been carved up by A-roads, and their trees, ancient as the hills, keep on quietly growing, untouched by the chaos of the world beyond the park boundaries.

Blenheim Palace's gorgeous Italian Garden

Blenheim Palace, Oxfordshire

As landscape architect Lancelot "Capability" Brown's biographer Dorothy Stroud puts it, "The park at Blenheim has always been regarded as the epitome of Brown's achievement, and there is no doubt that the honey-coloured mass of Vanbrugh's palace, set on the crest of high ground, proved a spur to his genius."

The house was given to John Churchill, 1st Duke of Marlborough, by Queen Anne following his victory at the Battle of Blenheim in 1704. By the 4th duke's tenure, it was time to redo the gardens. In 1763, the duke called in Brown to complete the landscaping around the palace. This had been designed in the early years of the 18th century by Sir John Vanbrugh, and already had a lake, a bridge and one long, straight avenue. Over the next decade, Brown would go on to build two dams and a further 40-acre lake, plant belts of trees around the park boundary, remodel the entrance to the north side of the palace, and design new drives and rides.

Later, the 9th Duke of Marlborough (1871-1934) described Brown's achievements at Blenheim: "The lake was made by a consummate artist. The contours are good, the ground has been made to undulate; a convex bank on one side finds its vis-a-vis with a concave bank on the other side. All this done with the skill of the Romantic period and on a scale bigger than the Bassin des Suisses [the Swiss pond at Versailles]."

Brown didn't just dig holes for lakes, but continued the 3rd duke's work in planting belts of trees around the edge of the estate, creating a double row – not just for privacy, but to give an illusion of a forest setting. Brown designed two drives into the park – one from the local town of Woodstock, with the house, lake and bridge coming into view across the valley; and another, more theatrical drive from the south, where the water could be glimpsed at different points through the trees. William Fordyce Mavor, tutor to the 4th duke's children, described these ever-changing views in a guidebook from the late 18th century: "The water, the palace, the gardens, the great bridge, the pillar, Woodstock, and other near and remote objects, open and shut upon the eye like enchantment."

Today, Blenheim Palace is the home of the 12th Duke of Marlborough and his family. Visits to Blenheim are ticketed, with an option to purchase a ticket for the house, gardens and park, or just for the gardens and park. Public access to the parkland is available free of charge from the centre of Woodstock town, via Chaucer's Lane, though access via the main entrance gives visitors the opportunity to explore Blenheim's wider offering. Woodstock is key to Blenheim, the palace's chief executive Dominic Hare says: "Woodstock predates Blenheim, and it has always been part of the umbilical relationship between the two. We feel very lucky that we're so close to such a nice town – we work hand in glove with the town to make sure that people who come to Blenheim are encouraged to enjoy Woodstock." **Blenheim Park, Woodstock OX20 1UL. 01993 810530; blenheimpalace.com**

Burghley's park hosts sheep and fallow deer

Capability Brown's Lion Bridge

Burghley House, Lincolnshire

The great gates appear, and the park opens up – first with sheep grazing, and then, as the path winds up the hill and through the deer gate, fallow deer dot the landscape. You can walk along this path for some time before the great Elizabethan edifice of Burghley House appears, home of the Cecil family for over 460 years.

The park at Burghley is, house director and granddaughter of the 6th Marquess of Exeter Miranda Rock says, integral to the local area. "The relationship between Burghley and Stamford is intimate. There is an arbitrary wall around the park, but it's pretty permeable.

Everybody who has learnt to ride a bike locally has pretty much done it here."

Burghley House was built by Sir William Cecil, later 1st Lord Burghley, in 1555 as an early "prodigy house" – one to impress Queen Elizabeth I – fittingly in an "E" shape. The park that welcomes visitors today is an 18th-century creation. In common with many stately homes of the time, Burghley had formal, intricate gardens. And then "Capability" Brown arrived with the 18th-century equivalent of a wrecking ball, and ripped it all out in favour of a more naturalistic landscape.

His association with Burghley began in 1754 when Brownlow Cecil, 9th Earl of Exeter, employed him to modernise the grounds.

At Burghley, his landscape hallmarks are plain to see. The lake, which is designed to look like a river, is made from a series of old stew ponds which were no doubt used by the first Lord Burghley for fresh supplies of fish. To go with the lake, Brown designed a stone bridge, the Lion Bridge, sending his drawings of it to Lord Exeter at the end of 1772. Later that year, the bridge was begun, being completed in spring 1777 when four lions in Coade stone were supplied. Brown wrote in 1778 that "This is a great place, where I have had twenty-five years' pleasure in restoring the monument of a great minister to a great Queen."

Today, the park is open free of charge daily from 7am until 6pm (unless dusk comes before), with dogs permitted on leads in the park, though not in the gardens, which, like the house, are ticketed.
Burghley House, Stamford PE9 3JY. 01780 752451; burghley.co.uk

Cirencester Park, Gloucestershire

The estate has been in the Bathurst family since 1695, when it was bought by Sir Benjamin Bathurst, a governor of the East India Company. Today's house, which is screened from the town by an enormous yew hedge, was built by Sir Benjamin's son Allen Bathurst, 1st Earl Bathurst, from 1714.

The park is very pretty indeed, and is open to everyone all year round, 8am until 5pm. It's only not open later because of the wildlife: "You've got deer out there with their young, badgers out with their cubs, and foxes, too. They've got to be left to have their peace and quiet, without humans stomping through their living room," Lady Bathurst told me. Visitors can walk, run, or ride horses in the park, but not cycle. Well-behaved dogs are permitted on leads.

When the 1st Earl Bathurst inherited Cirencester Park in 1704, he set about rebuilding the 16th-century house. Later acquiring the neighbouring Sapperton Estate, he considered how he would design the park, and joined forces with his friend English poet Alexander Pope, an expert on the Ancient Roman and Greek classical landscapes. The pair were members of the Kit-Cat Club, a political group who had the architect of Blenheim Palace, Sir John Vanbrugh, among its members. Lord Bathurst designed his park with deer hunting in mind, and there is a variety of spaces: wooded areas to the north and west, and more open spaces to the south-west.

The park was conceived at a time when geometric avenues were beginning to look old-fashioned. A new, more naturalistic approach was on the rise, pre-dating the influence of "Capability" Brown. Pope wrote in the autumn of 1718: "I am with Lord Bathurst in my bower, in whose groves we yesterday had a dry walk of three hours. It is the place of all others that I fancy." With Bathurst he pondered schemes "to open avenues, cut glades, plant firs, contrive waterworks, all very fine and beautiful in our imagination".

And it wasn't just avenues and lakes Lord Bathurst was interested in. The park contains a number of garden buildings. The limestone, six-sided hexagon folly is also Grade II listed, while Alfred's Hall is a Gothic sham ruin, probably the first of these built in England.

Pope's Seat is a Grade II listed neoclassical building with iron seats and pedimented arches, named in honour of Lord Bathurst's friend. And then there's Queen Anne's Monument, built in 1741 to commemorate the monarch. Some 50-feet high, it is a giant Doric column crowned with a statue of the queen.

Bathurst lived to be 91, dying in 1775. Some time before, when he was in his 80s, the writer Sir Horace Walpole described Bathurst as one "with philosophic calmness, [in] the shade of those trees which he himself had planted half a century before". **Bathurst, Park St, Cirencester GL7 2BU. 01285 653135; bathurstestate.co.uk**

Pope's Seat, named for Alexander Pope

Cirencester Park is screened by a massive yew hedge built by the 1st Earl Bathurst in 1714

Images: Alamy, Shutterstock

ICE IN THE COCKPIT

Roger Harvey celebrates daring British aviators Alcock and Brown, who achieved the first non-stop flight across the Atlantic

EVERYONE knew the Atlantic was a dangerous ocean, but since ancient times it had held a fascination as a vast space: explored by the earliest sailors, later crossed by Vikings, Columbus, pioneer settlers, and centuries of traffic between Europe and America.

Ships of all types braved its storms, fogs and ice, but if 20th-century technology had appeared to tame it, the shocking loss of the *Titanic* proved that disaster and tragedy could still haunt this awesome ocean.

Every Atlantic crossing was fraught with risk; to attempt a crossing by air seemed sheer madness. But this was 1919. The Great War had produced swift developments in aviation and, as peacetime dawned, a generation of brave and daring aviators was ready to blaze new trails in the sky, break records and inspire an enthralled public.

Ever since 1909, when Louis Blériot had crossed the English Channel in his flimsy monoplane, daring pilots were focusing their ambitions on wider stretches of water. The greatest achievement would be the Atlantic, non-stop. And there was a prize: the then enormous sum of £10,000 was put up by the *Daily Mail*.

Several teams backed by major aircraft manufacturers laid their plans, assembled equipment, and sought the best pilots.

The Mancunian John Alcock and the Scot Arthur Whitten Brown were both veteran flyers of the Great War. Each, in separate incidents, had been shot down and taken prisoner. Safely back home, they met at Brooklands, that cradle of aviation and motor sport, where Alcock was working for Vickers, whose aircraft division was making a bid for the transatlantic prize. His enthusiasm had secured him the position of pilot.

Brown turned up for a job interview. When asked if he could

Opposite: The Vickers Vimy biplane in a bog in Galway, where it landed after the triumphant 16-hour flight. This page from left: John Alcock and Arthur Whitten Brown with a model of their plane and the bag of mail they carried on the flight; the front page of The New York Times

navigate the Atlantic he simply said, "Yes", and found himself appointed as navigator to Alcock.

The aircraft chosen by the Vickers team was the Vickers Vimy, a heavy bomber whose prototype first flew in 1917. Intended to carry a large bomb-load deep into Germany, it only entered service at the very end of the war and never carried out that role, although it continued a successful career with the RAF into the 1930s.

While still an example of early aircraft construction using wood and fabric, the Vimy was a safe and steady flyer with, as pilots say, "plenty of wing" to give good lift and stability at various speeds and in adverse conditions.

It was driven by two powerful Rolls-Royce Eagle engines, which had been designed by Henry Royce himself, and had proved to be robust and reliable in other aircraft during the war.

The Atlantic Vimy was adapted by Vickers to fly even farther than its original long range: the bomb racks carried vast fuel tanks. But with a cockpit open to the elements and only the simplest navigational aids, Alcock and Brown would have none of the comfort and security taken for granted when flying the Atlantic today.

Arriving at St. John's in Newfoundland, Canada, Alcock and Brown found the rival Handley Page team already testing their aircraft but pre-occupied with final adjustments and awaiting perfect conditions. The Vickers men saw an opportunity to beat their rival and lost no time in getting airborne.

Alcock and Brown took off in the early afternoon of 14 June, 1919, their heavily laden Vimy struggling into the sky and just clearing a row of trees at the end of the field. On board they had 865 gallons of fuel, packets of sandwiches, chocolate and coffee, bottles of beer, and their two toy cat mascots named Lucky Jim and Twinkletoes.

They also carried what would become the first transatlantic air-mail, including Alcock's handwritten note to his sister. Almost a century later this would turn up on *Antiques Roadshow* and be valued at £1,200.

Almost from the start the flight was bedevilled by ill luck and a series of setbacks that threatened to end in disaster.

Within hours they encountered impenetrable fog. Brown could not use his sextant to fix a position and with no gyroscopic instruments it was almost impossible to keep a straight or level course. When they entered a huge cumulonimbus cloud, the violent storm it contained spun the Vimy into a spiral dive from which Alcock only just recovered in time. A trim control broke which meant the aircraft would become nose-heavy as fuel was consumed and Alcock would have to exert increasing effort to haul her away from the waves below.

Even more drastic than this was the failure of their wind-driven generator. Now they had no intercom, no radio, and no power for their electrically heated flying-suits. A terrible coldness soaked into the men, made less bearable by the lashing of freezing rain. When a cracked exhaust pipe was swept off in the slipstream, they were deafened by a relentless roar coming from only a few feet from their heads.

OTHER PIONEERING FLIGHTS

Alcock and Brown's was just one of the daring achievements made by aviation pioneers. Here are some of the others:

17 December 1903 American brothers Wilbur and Orville Wright made the first successful flight in history when their gas-powered, propeller-driven biplane remained airborne for 12 seconds, flying over 120 feet of North Carolina soil. In a later attempt that day, the plane stayed in the air for 59 seconds, covering 852 feet. The age of aviation was born.

21 May 1927 Charles Lindbergh landed in the record books when he completed the first nonstop, solo transatlantic flight. He landed at the Le Bourget airfield in Paris in his Spirit of St Louis, single-engine monoplane after setting off from Long Island, New York, 33½ hours earlier, covering 3,600 miles in the process.

21 May 1933 Exactly five years after Lindberg, American pilot Amelia Earhart became the second person and the first woman to fly nonstop over the Atlantic. Flying, like Alcock and Brown, from Newfoundland to Ireland, she completed the 2,000 mile journey in just under 15 hours.

A monument to the flight, close to where the plane landed in Galway

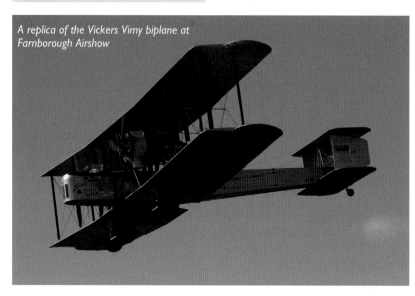

A replica of the Vickers Vimy biplane at Farnborough Airshow

For a while the skies cleared and Brown could use the stars to confirm they were on course, but later they flew into a severe snowstorm. Their instruments were frozen up and the aircraft wings developed a disastrous load of ice. Ice also began to choke the air-intakes and carburettors, threatening to kill the engines.

In an act of desperate bravery later dismissed as fiction invented by the press (for, in true stiff-upper-lip fashion, Brown never talked of it), the frozen, deafened and wind-blasted navigator clambered out on to the wings to hack away the ice and save themselves from certain death in the hopeless waters below.

At last they headed into a clearer dawn, and the coast of Ireland rode up over the eastern horizon. Amazingly, after a numbing 16 hours in the air, Brown had navigated them to within a few miles of their intended landfall near Clifden in County Galway.

Relieved and exultant, Alcock set down on what looked like a smooth green field. Alas, this turned out to be the notorious Derrigimlagh Bog, into which the Vimy dug her nose. There was some damage to the aircraft but no one was hurt. Alcock remarked drily that they'd have been better off carrying on to London, which they would have done had they not been so cold.

Of course, Alcock and Brown became instant heroes, claiming the *Daily Mail* prize for Britain and for Vickers and being awarded large sums of money themselves. On their return to London they were knighted by George V, celebrated in a speech by Winston Churchill at a dinner at the Savoy, and treated to a civic reception when they returned to Manchester.

Eight years later, Charles Lindbergh would be first to fly the Atlantic solo and attract arguably greater fame, yet he was gracious enough to admit that Alcock and Brown had been the courageous trail-blazers.

Clockwise from top left: The plane prior to take off; final preparations underway; Alcock and Brown reading the headlines on the deck of a ship taking them from Ireland back to England following their victorious flight; Pilot John William Alcock; Navigator Arthur Whitten Brown

Today the famous Vickers Vimy can be seen at the Science Museum in Kensington. There has been a statue of Alcock and Brown at London's Heathrow Airport since the 1950s. It shows them in full flying kit, looking at each other in brotherly fashion, perhaps about to take off for another exploit. It is a somehow poignant work.

These old heroes are long dead and perhaps forgotten by many, but their spirit of adventure and determination should fly with every jet taking heedless passengers in comfort and safety across the unforgiving and deadly expanse of the Atlantic Ocean.

I remember, growing up as a child of the "jet age" in the 1950s and '60s, being enthralled by the aircraft of my own time. They were sleek and beautiful and capable of seemingly endless advances in speed and luxury, but it was the daring of the early aviators before, during and after the Great War which captured my imagination more deeply.

These men and women were closer to the elements through which they flew and in very "hands-on" contact with their comparatively primitive machines. They explored the first unknowns of air travel, displaying at times unbelievable courage in the face of extraordinary challenges.

Between the solo exploits of Blériot and Lindbergh, no one exemplifies the excitement of courageous teamwork more dramatically than John Alcock and Arthur Whitten Brown.

Winston Churchill hands over the £10,000 winners' cheque

Images: Shutterstock

The Morning Sun

by George Hughes

The brilliant sun of early morn
That blinding light as day is born,
Golden yellow intense delight
Now dawn has rolled away dark night.

I stand in awe, such a wondrous scene,
'Neath a sky of blue in fields of green.
I feel the radiance warm my face,
Arising at such a gentle pace.

I realise now why ancient man
Worshipped the sun as bare he ran,
Across the earth whilst down it shone
Then hid in caves when it was gone.
But now we know that God, through you,
Gives life to all, blest orb so true.

Image: Shutterstock

Mullion Cove on the Lizard Peninsula, Cornwall

SPRING TO SUMMER

Flower shows, the summer solstice, discover Cornwall's magnificent gardens and dive into the chilly history of seabathing >

SPRING TO SUMMER

As the days lengthen, festivals, flower shows and sporting events all make a rich season of events, says Katherine Sorrell

THE 150TH ANNIVERSARY OF THE FOUNDING OF THE KENNEL CLUB

The Kennel Club was the first official registry of purebred dogs in the world, set up on 4 April, 1873, by MP and dog breeder Sewallis Shirley and a group of like-minded gentlemen. Their aim was to establish a consistent set of rules for dog shows and field trials, with dog welfare in mind.

1876 engraving of Kennel Club winners

LONDON HARNESS HORSE PARADE

Every Easter Monday at the South of England Centre in Ardingly, West Sussex, an impressive parade of harness horses, ponies and donkeys offers a glimpse into a world gone by, showing how everything from eggs to beer was once transported. Expect more than 100 horse-drawn vehicles and carriages, from Shetlands to magnificent Shires. **lhhp.co.uk**

George VI in 1948

75 YEARS OF THE LAND ROVER

Basic but tough and designed for all terrains, the Land Rover was designed to be Britain's answer to the Jeep. It was unveiled by Rover at the Amsterdam Motor Show on 30 April 1948.

HAPPY 70TH BIRTHDAY, MR BOND

Ian Fleming's *Casino Royale*, featuring James Bond, Vesper Lynd and Le Chiffre, was published on 13 April 1953. It was an instant hit, and the former naval officer wrote 12 Bond novels in total – as well as the children's classic *Chitty Chitty Bang Bang*.

ROYAL MAUNDY SERVICE

On the Thursday before Easter (April 6 in 2023), the reigning monarch distributes special Maundy money to local pensioners in recognition of their contribution to community and to the church. The Royal Maundy Service, which dates back to 600AD, takes place at a different cathedral or abbey each year. Each recipient is given two small leather purses, one red and one white. The first contains a small amount of ordinary coinage that symbolises the Sovereign's gift for food and clothing, while the second contains Maundy coins up to the value of the Sovereign's age. Participation is by invitation only, but anyone may watch outside. **royal.uk/maundy-thursday**

WORLD COAL CARRYING CHAMPIONSHIPS

It began with a challenge in the pub. Sixty years later, it has become another of England's inimitable and quirky traditions: the World Coal Carrying Championships, in which men and women race the streets of the West Yorkshire village of Gawthorpe carrying heavy sacks of coal (50kg and 20kg respectively), every Easter Monday. **gawthorpemaypole.org.uk**

Laden with coal in the ladies race in 1967

THE GRAND NATIONAL

The Grand National is best known for the four-mile steeplechase that is the ultimate challenge in jumps racing. However, it is in fact a three-day festival held at Aintree Racecourse in Merseyside, with the first day a relaxed day of racing and entertainment, while the second, Ladies Day, brings the spotlight on fashion and extraordinary hats! In the exciting finale of the Grand National itself, 40 horses and riders jump 30 notoriously difficult fences over two laps of the Aintree course. **thejockeyclub.co.uk**

MALDON MUD RACE

This mad, mud bath-cum-charity fundraiser takes place on a Sunday in late April or early May in the Essex town of Maldon. It has been going since the 1970s. Described as "fun with a competitive edge", it draws crowds in the tens of thousands to watch competitors, often in fancy dress, make their way through the deep, thick mud of the Blackwater Estuary, on a challenging 400m course. Entry to watch in Promenade Park is by donation and there are huge TV screens that capture every muddy moment. There are also stalls, refreshments, activities and other entertainment during the day. **maldonmudrace.com**

BATH COMEDY FESTIVAL

This springtime extravaganza of laughs usually runs for almost three weeks over late March and early April at venues around the Georgian city of Bath. Featuring household names and newcomers alike, the festival's aim is to bring Bath to life with a vibrant mix of comedy in all its guises. **bathcomedy.com**

FRITILLARY SUNDAY

The rare snake's head fritillary flower is found only in a handful of places in southern England and the Midlands. Ducklington, Oxfordshire is the only place in England where it is possible to walk among the flowers – for just one day a year. On Fritillary Sunday the 10-acre meadow is opened to the public, who may also enjoy ploughman's lunches and cream teas, Morris dancing, handbell ringing and a large plant stall, with all proceeds going to Ducklington Church. **ducklingtonchurch.org.uk**

A snake's head fritillary

ST GEORGE'S DAY

A feast day of Saint George has been celebrated in England on 23 April for centuries. In the Middle Ages George was believed to be one of a group of saints who could help during an epidemic. Shakespeare had Henry V calling on Saint George in his famous battle speech ("God for Harry, England and Saint George!") and his image is on many World War I memorials. Events take place up and down the country, notably in London's Trafalgar Square. **london.gov.uk**

CUCKOO DAY

Cuckoo Fair in Heathfield, East Sussex, dates back to 1315, when cuckoos were released at the start of spring. It has craft stalls, displays, vintage cars and a dog show, all raising money for charity. At Marsden, West Yorkshire, the celebration has workshops, a craft fair, dancing and a procession led by a giant wicker-and-paper cuckoo. **facebook.com/hefflecuckoofair1315; facebook. com/MarsdenCuckoo**

THE 80TH ANNIVERSARY OF THE "DAM BUSTERS"

Dramatised in the 1955 movie *The Dam Busters*, Operation Chastise (as it was officially called) was an audacious wartime raid against the German industrial heartland of the Ruhr Valley. On the night of 16-17 May 1943, the RAF's 617 Squadron flew low over enemy territory and released a series of "bouncing bombs", designed to bounce over anti-torpedo nets and destroy three dams. Two were breached and one was damaged. Catastrophic flooding ensued, numerous factories were destroyed, and the Nazi war effort had to be diverted from coastal defences to rebuilding the dams. The mission was hailed at the time as a triumphant success, though 53 of the 133 airmen involved died in the mission, and around 1,600 civilians and prisoners of war were drowned.

LICHFIELD BOWER

Not many community festivals can claim a history all the way back to 1145. Lichfield's spring bank holiday Monday event dates back to Henry II's demands for an annual muster of fighting men; in this case, they were assembled before magistrates at a "bower house" decorated with laurel and lilac, given free beef and wine and then paraded around the city. These days, there's still a procession, now with bands and floats, plus a humorous "court of arraye", fairground attractions, arts and crafts, food and market stalls, and live music. **lichfieldbower.co.uk**

TETBURY WOOLSACK RACES

Much like the coal carrying championships, in Gawthorpe (see March, p37), the Woolsack Races in the Cotswold town of Tetbury involve men and women running up a one-in-four hill carrying a heavy weight – in this case, a specially made sack of wool (60lb for men and 35lb for women). The event celebrates Tetbury's heritage as a market for wool, and has also been a fun family day out for more than 30 years, also featuring a street fair, fun fair, live music and roving entertainers. **tetburywoolsack.co.uk**

GLYNDEBOURNE FESTIVAL

The summer season of world-class opera in the heart of the Sussex countryside begins in May. The festival has a tradition of formal dress, with audiences donning their finery and enjoying the 90-minute interval with a picnic in the gardens. **glyndebourne.com**

Picnicking in the grounds of Glyndebourne

ROYAL WINDSOR HORSE SHOW

Taking place in the private grounds of Windsor Castle, top equestrian sport on offer at the UK's largest outdoor horse show includes international showjumping and dressage along with a host of showing classes. Don't miss the much-loved Shetland Pony Grand National, Land Rover International Driving Grand Prix, and the Household Cavalry's Musical Ride, with their iconic flag charge home. **rwhs.co.uk**

HAMLET AT THE AGE OF 75

On 4 May 1948, Sir Laurence Olivier's film of *Hamlet* was released. Renowned as the most compelling version of the tragedy, it went on to be the first British film to win the Academy Award for Best Picture.

Sir Laurence as Hamlet

BRISTOL WALK FEST

One of the UK's largest urban celebrations of walking, held in Bristol, during the National Walking Month of May, enjoy historical tours, nature walks, explorations of street art, wild food forays, walking sports tasters and more. **bristolwalkfest.com**

BATH FESTIVAL

Bath's flagship festival of music and literature brings world-class artists and authors to the Georgian city and is accompanied by a Fringe Festival covering myriad art forms. It all ends with a Finale Weekend that's a family-friendly showcase of live music. **bathfestivals.org.uk**

COOPERS HILL CHEESE ROLLING

Roll with it . . . Coopers Hill in Gloucestershire

What do you get when you combine the spring bank holiday, a very steep hill and a huge great wheel of Double Gloucester? The answer is this world-famous, somewhat bizarre and really quite dangerous event at Brockworth, Gloucestershire. The cheese reaches astonishing speeds of more than 70mph (and it's not unheard of for some entrants to be hospitalised) but if you're the winner you get to keep it! Enter very much at your own risk.
visitgloucester.co.uk

THE ALRESFORD WATERCRESS FESTIVAL

Watercress takes centre-stage in the Hampshire town of Alresford on the third Sunday of May each year. The Georgian market town was built from the riches of the watercress industry, even boasting its own steam railway nicknamed the Watercress Line (now a working heritage attraction). A huge street festival includes food and craft stalls, live music, cookery, children's activities and a parade. The piece de resistance is The World Watercress Eating Championships.
watercressfestival.org

CRAB AND LOBSTER FESTIVAL

Two of Norfolk's popular seaside destinations, Cromer and Sheringham, get together in a lively celebration of their seafaring heritage. The event starts off with a variety concert, and features heritage demonstrations, a cookery theatre, the "Bootiful" Boat Art Trail and the Scrumptious Seafood Trail, plus live music, a street market packed with local produce, heritage and seafaring crafts and children's activities.
crabandlobsterfestival.co.uk

RHS CHELSEA FLOWER SHOW

The world's most prestigious flower show brings together extraordinary show gardens, floral displays and great shopping over five days at the Royal Hospital, Chelsea. Get expert advice, spot trends, see cutting-edge garden design and sip champagne while admiring incredible horticultural creativity. **rhs.org.uk**

Inside the floral Marquee at Chelsea

BRIGHTON FESTIVALS

If you head down to the south coast in May you will be treated to an array of festivals in and around the seaside city of Brighton. There's the Brighton Festival itself, a three-week celebration of music, theatre, dance, circus, art, film and literature that's been running since 1967, and is the largest annual curated multi-arts festival in England. Then there's the huge, open-access Brighton Fringe, which embraces every art form and artistic expression, with hundreds of different events. Every weekend there's Artists Open Houses, in which more than 1,000 local artists open their homes to exhibit their work and sell directly to their visitors. And The Great Escape is a festival for new music, showcasing more than 400 up-and-coming artists from all over the world. Last but not least, at nearby Charleston, the modernist home and studio of painters Vanessa Bell and Duncan Grant, its festival brings together artists, writers, thinkers and changemakers, with an eye to challenging the status-quo and daring to imagine society differently – just as the Bloomsbury Group did around the Charleston dining room table 100 years ago. **visitbrighton.com/whats-on/festivals**

Brighton's landmark Pavilion

GOODWOOF

Billed as "the world's most spectacular dog event", Goodwoof is a grand celebration of all things dog, including competitions and demonstrations, dog wellness and family fun. Taking place at The Kennels at Goodwood, West Sussex, it's a unique experience for dog lovers. **goodwood.com/goodwoof**

>

THE ART AND ANTIQUES FAIR

The capital's highly respected Art and Antiques Fair boasts displays by the finest specialist dealers, who offer a wide choice of high quality, vetted art and antiques. The fair attracts enthusiasts from around the world to Olympia looking for that inspirational, unique piece, whether modern and eclectic or traditional and classic. **olympia-art-antiques.com**

Emma Raducanu on court

THE CHAMPIONSHIPS, WIMBLEDON

It began with 22 amateur tennis players who answered an ad in the leisure magazine *The Field* in June 1877. They each paid 11 shillings to take part, with a final played in front of 200 people. These days, the attendance is more than 500,000, with a TV audience of millions and prize money totalling almost £40m. This year's tournament takes place from 26 June to 9 July. Who's for a Pimm's? **wimbledon.com**

HANDMADE OXFORD

The International Contemporary Arts Festival takes place at the beautiful Waterperry Gardens, Oxford, with a host of appealing crafts, workshops and demonstrations, in a celebration of art, craft, design, sculpture and artisan food. **handmadeinbritain.co.uk**

EPSOM DERBY

One of our great national sporting events, the Derby is run over a distance of 1 mile, 4 furlongs and 10 yards and is open only to three-year-old colts and fillies. Alongside the racing, expect lots of dressing up, picnics, live music and other entertainment. **thejockeyclub.co.uk**

COTSWOLD OLIMPICK GAMES

The first Cotswold Olimpicks – described by the British Olympic Association as beginning the historical thread in Britain that led to the creation of the modern Olympics – were probably held in 1612. They were organised by lawyer Robert Dover just outside the town of Chipping Campden in the Cotswolds. Core activities were athletics, throwing, jumping, wrestling and horse racing, and at some point traditional Cotswold wrestling developed into a localised version known as shin kicking. Revived in the 1960s, the games have run almost every year since, and are now a unique event that includes the World Shin Kicking Championships (which is as it sounds!) and other early rural sporting competitions, including Tug o' War, running races and King of the Hill, an antecedent of the pentathlon. **olimpickgames.co.uk**

THE ELGAR FESTIVAL

Held annually around the weekend closest to Elgar's birthday (2 June 1857), this musical celebration of our greatest composer, based in and near his home town of Worcester, combines an ambitious programme of concerts, workshops and recitals with educational opportunities and community projects. **elgarfestival.org**

BOVEY TRACEY CRAFT FESTIVAL

Hundreds of designer-maker stands, hand-picked for quality, are the heart of this annual three-day festival in Bovey Tracey, Devon, while alongside are workshops and demonstrations, live music and locally sourced food. **craftfestival.co.uk**

ROYAL ASCOT

A highlight of the summer social season, Royal Ascot is about making a style statement as much as the horse racing. The five-day meeting attracts many of the world's finest thoroughbreds, which compete for more than £8m in prize money. The Royal Procession at 2pm, when the Royal Family's horse-drawn carriages approach along the famous Straight Mile, marks the start of each race day. **ascot.com**

THE GREAT KNARESBOROUGH BED RACE

About 90 teams race to raise money for good causes along a gruelling 2.4 mile course around the North Yorkshire town of Knaresborough that includes steep slopes, cobbles and an icy swim at the end. The twist? They're all pushing a wheeled "bed" and a passenger. As well as the time trial, there's also a splendid fancy-dress procession with prizes. **bedrace.co.uk**

GOLOWAN

Cornish towns once honoured Midsummer with bonfires, flaming tar barrels and burning torches – until the late 19th century, when the perceived fire risk made insurance premiums too high. In 1991, however, the town of Penzance revived the tradition. The event has now grown into a ten-day community-led extravaganza, with a serpent dance, Mock Mayor Election, quayside fair, talks, workshops and a fireworks display. On Mazey Day, the final Saturday, a series of parades – featuring giant sculptures, singing, dancing and bands – are watched by tens of thousands of locals and visitors. **golowanfestival.org**

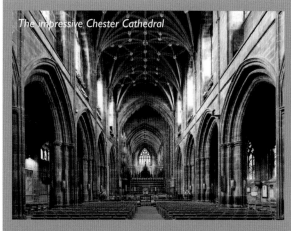
The impressive Chester Cathedral

CHESTER MYSTERY PLAYS

The Chester Mystery Plays, based on well-known Bible stories including the Nativity, Noah's Ark and the Crucifixion, originated in the 14th century. Banned in 1578, they were revived as part of the 1951 Festival of Britain celebrations, and their modern-day performance is a highly anticipated five-yearly event. They are produced (under professional direction) by the people of Chester, and attract visitors from all over the world. The next cycle will be performed in Chester Cathedral from 28 June-15 July. **chestermysteryplays.com**

ROYAL ACADEMY SUMMER EXHIBITION

Anyone can enter their works of art into the Royal Academy's Summer Exhibition, which features art created by everyone from emerging artists to the biggest names in art and architecture. Many of the galleries in Burlington House in London are hung densely, high and low, while some are dedicated to a single artist. Others feature film, photography or installations. **royalacademy.org.uk**

The Royal Academy's Summer Exhibition

SUMMER SOLSTICE

Marking the end of spring and the beginning of summer, the longest day of the year in 2023 falls on 21 June and will be celebrated all over the country by Druids, Pagans and lovers of nature alike. Probably the best-known destination is Stonehenge, in Wiltshire, whose sarsen stones, erected in the centre of the site in about 2,500 BC, were carefully positioned to line up with the movements of the sun. Its first rays shine from behind the Heel Stone, the ancient entrance to the stone circle, and into the heart of the prehistoric World Heritage Site. English Heritage provides free, managed open access to the site for individuals and groups and booking is essential. Not far from Stonehenge, Avebury Henge is the world's largest prehistoric stone circle. Normally much quieter than Stonehenge, Avebury

Sun salutations at Stonehenge

becomes busy at solstice times as people gather to celebrate the time of new beginnings. And at Glastonbury Tor in Somerset, a landmark steeped in history and legend, crowds gather to drum and chant at sunrise and generally welcome the longest day. **english-heritage.org.uk; nationaltrust.org. uk/glastonbury-tor**

Images: Shutterstock/Alamy

LIVERPOOL CASTLE REPLICA

Lord Leverhulme's unfinished folly in Lever Park
near Bolton gives Chris Franks pause for thought

The castle replica was never completed, and is now falling down

HOW to describe Liverpool Castle Replica? That's the name of the bizarre structure overlooking Rivington Reservoir in Lever Park, near Bolton. It's an odd combination, a fragment of a replica of a ruin.

The original Liverpool Castle used to stand in the centre of Liverpool, on what is now Derby Square. It was built in the early 13th century, and by 1726 had completely disappeared. The construction at Rivington was intended to be a scale replica of that castle – not as it stood in its heyday, but of when it was in ruin. The building work began in 1912, but was never finished.

When you first see it, it doesn't feel like something old. There's no sense of history or past life. The courtyard looks like industrial estate scrubland, with coarse grass, tangles of brambles and tracks of bare earth that recent rain has pitted with large puddles. The walls are incomplete, but all the corners and edges of the stone blocks are still sharp. The place feels more like a building site with construction temporarily halted.

It was the creation of William Hesketh Lever, also known as Lord Leverhulme, and was intended to be the principal feature of a park for the people of Bolton. Lever was a hugely successful businessman and generous philanthropist. He established the global corporation known today as Unilever, and served as MP for the Wirral, later sitting in the House of Lords. He founded schools, museums and art galleries, and he donated land and valuable artworks for public enjoyment. He was a big man with big ideas.

Alongside this, the replica seems insignificant. After 13 years of construction, all work ceased on it when Lever died in 1925. Considering everything else Lever achieved, this is strange. Surely a man like him could have got the job done in just a few months? It's as if he was keen initially, but then lost interest.

As you wander around, you can sense this. The place has an air of the rejected lover, as if one moment it was thriving in the glow of Lever's affection, and the next left hurt and puzzled when that affection turned cold. And yet there is a lingering sense of hope, too, that maybe, in time, building work will resume.

But this place doesn't have time. Signs everywhere ask people not to climb because it is damaging the walls. Pieces of litter lie snagged in the brambles and, in the enclosed spaces, graffiti artists have been having fun. Fresh ivy is spreading everywhere, and with gaps between the blocks big enough for your fingertips, its destructive work won't take long.

How to describe Liverpool Castle Replica? Maybe as the doomed remnant of a passing fancy, still waiting for Lever's passion to return and for a day of fulfilment that will never come.

Stunning borders as well as sculpture

TREMENHEERE SCULPTURE GARDENS

These fascinating gardens are on land that was held by the monks of St Michael's Mount until 1295, when Michael De Tremenheere bought it. In the family for around 600 years, Seymour, the last Tremenheere to own it, planted holly, beech, sweet chestnut and oak trees around 1830, and shaped what the gardens look like today. A breathtaking location for a garden, the sheltered valley overlooks the sea, with St Michael's Mount visible in the distance. It's a modern garden with contemporary artwork and sculpture finding homes amongst sub-tropical and exotic specimens. Bamboo, succulents and palm trees grow well here, as the temperatures in winter aren't too severe and the area's sheltered from extreme wind. The site is home to evolving exhibitions of art, having featured artists such as David Nash and James Turrell. If you are after something different in a garden visit, something modern yet in tune with the landscape (and with a spectacular view), then Tremenheere could be one for you. **Tremenheere Sculpture Garden, Gulval, Penzance, Cornwall TR20 8YL. 01736 448089; tremenheere.co.uk**

GAP/Carole Drake

CORNWALL'S GLORIOUS GARDENS

Alice Johnson recommends a visit in the summer

THE sun's high in the sky, flickering through the gaps in the palm leaves that move in the breeze. It's like a jungle here. There's the sound of water running from a nearby stream, too, and wherever you turn there is dense green growth. While it feels like I've travelled far, I am in fact on British soil. That's the magic of a well-crafted garden: each space takes you to a specific part of the world. And while Cornwall is desired for its coastline, head inland a little and some of the gardens are just as spectacular. With its warmer climate, plants are grown here that might struggle elsewhere. Here are some of my favourite gardens.　　>

Howard Rice

EDEN PROJECT

Opened in 2001, the white biomes of the Eden Project, in an old clay pit, make it one of the most recognisable sites in the UK, and you'll need a day to explore. In the Rainforest Biome there's a rise in temperature as it houses plants from tropical South America to South-East Asia and West Africa, along with crops like coffee, vanilla and oil palm. There are waterfalls and a canopy route with spectacular views. There are bamboos, palms, bananas, pineapples and birds like roul-roul partridges that live here. Particularly interesting is the carnivorous highland tropical pitcher plant as it catches insects and is not usually seen outside Borneo and Sumatra.

The Mediterranean Biome is home to plants from the Mediterranean Basin, South Africa, California and Western Australia, with crops including grapes, cork and cotton. Look for bird of paradise plants, olive trees, aloe and the enticing perfume garden. Outside, the gardens are just as strong, with vegetables and flowers, which in summer include lavender and dahlias. Bombus the Giant Bee sculpture, created by Robert Bradford, is surrounded by blooms and buzzing bees at this time of year, too.

The Eden Project has the "wow" factor and makes you think about the world itself. As you explore, you'll learn how ecosystems support us and how important it is to protect them for the future.
Eden Project, Bodelva, Cornwall PL24 2SG. 01726 811972; edenproject.com

The Rainforest Biome at the Eden Project

The lake in the Jungle area at Heligan

Tree ferns line a woodland path

GAP/John Glover

> ### THE LOST GARDENS OF HELIGAN

Perhaps one of the greatest horticultural stories of recent times was the rediscovery of Heligan's gardens. When World War I broke out, staff at the estate left to join the war effort, giving nature time to take over. In 1990 the garden was rediscovered, and what followed, thanks to Tim Schmidt, was one of the biggest garden restoration schemes in Europe.

Today, visitors can absorb the romance and adventure of Heligan's history when they venture into the steep-sided valley. Here, the Jungle sees exotic plants grow thanks to the warm microclimate. Follow the boardwalk through the greenery, bamboo and past the lakes. You can try the rope bridge and see giant rhubarb plants, bananas, palms and a New Zealand yew tree.

Stroll around the Pleasure Grounds, including the Italian, Sundial, New Zealand and Sikkim garden areas. Some beautiful features here are the Kitchen Garden, Flower Garden and Melon Yard, including the famous Pineapple Pit. Vegetables, flowers, herbs, fruit and salads grow, which are supplied to the café on site. The Productive Gardens are an homage to previous gardeners'

horticultural legacies. You will find the Thunderbox Room here, now a living memorial, where Victorian gardeners signed their names. Summer is a romantic season in the gardens, and with the estate to see, too, including meadows and woodlands, leave yourself the day to explore.
The Lost Gardens of Heligan, Pentewan, St Austell, Cornwall PL26 6EN. 01726 845100; heligan.com

Agapanthus and hydrangeas

TREBAH GARDEN

Head to the Water Garden to see white arum lilies and yellow-red spikes of ginger lilies in late summer. Further highlights include the Bamboozle, a maze-like pathway of bamboo, Hydrangea Valley and South American plants in the Chilean Coomb. A highlight is the Gunnera Passage where gunnera or giant rhubarb have taken over. At the foot of this stunning 26-acre garden you'll find the beautiful Polgwidden Cove. **Trebah Garden Trust, Mawnan Smith, near Falmouth, Cornwall TR11 5JZ. 01326 252200; trebahgarden.co.uk**

GLENDURGAN GARDEN

The maze is a much-loved feature of this spectacular garden that was given to the National Trust in 1962. The land was purchased by Alfred Fox in 1823, and in 1833 the maze was planted. There's also a School Room here, rebuilt in 2001/2, inspired by the original building used to educate the Fox children.

In summer you're welcomed by floral borders filled with lush greens and seasonal blooms. Notice the Agave Americana, with fleshy, spiky-edged leaves as you make your way to the valleys. There are three valleys here, featuring exotic specimens like banana plants, tree ferns, bamboo and giant rhubarb. Historically, Alfred and his wife were keen to create shelterbelts for the garden, perfect for exotic specimens to flourish. There is a special tulip tree here, Liriodendron tulipifera, which was planted around 1830 and blooms in summer with lime green-orange flowers. Walk to the end of the garden and you'll reach the hamlet of Durgan and the Helford River. Glendurgan combines both waterside and horticultural beauty. **Glendurgan Garden, Mawnan Smith, near Falmouth, Cornwall TR11 5JZ. 01326 252020; nationaltrust.org.uk/glendurgan-garden** >

The maze at Glendurgan

TRELISSICK

Follow the meandering pathways to enjoy this garden with colour-filled borders and stunning maritime views over the Fal Estuary. Owned by the National Trust, there's a house at the centre (not always open) that leads onto the terrace and gardens.

The tower in the gardens

Admire the bold colours of salvias with their frenzy of bees as you enter, follow the Hydrangea Walk to reach the Tennis Lawn with glorious views, then on to Jack's Summerhouse.

When you reach the main lawn, the deep borders are rich with flowers, such as ginger lilies, along with exotic plants like bananas. The most characteristic aspect of this area is the huge Japanese red cedar, *Cryptomeria japonica*, that grows in the centre of the short-cut lawn. It is more than 100 years old. Another interesting part of the garden is the orchard where different apple varieties grow.

Along with the garden, there is the wider estate to explore, and with more than 300 acres there are many paths to choose from. You can, for example, follow a walking trail to Roundwood Quay, where you can also discover a nearby Iron Age promontory fort.

Trelissick, Feock, near Truro, Cornwall TR3 6QL. 01872 862090; nationaltrust.org.uk/ trelissick

The late spring garden at Lanhydrock

LANHYDROCK

This Victorian house at Lanhydrock is surrounded by a beautiful garden and estate. Run by the National Trust, the gardens boast formal parterres and herbaceous borders.

At Borlase's stream, which is named after a gardener who worked here for over 25 years, you can see red-orange blooms of crocosmia along with pink-red flowers of astilbes. There are summer-loving plants such as agapanthus and dahlias blooming in the garden.

With a glorious garden, exquisite house and around 900 acres of countryside to explore, there is something for all visitors to enjoy.
Lanhydrock, Bodmin, Cornwall PL30 4AB. 01208 265950; nationaltrust.org.uk/lanhydrock

A garden of trees in late spring/early summer

TREWITHEN GARDENS

The name Trewithen means "house of the trees" – an apt translation for this estate purchased by Phillip Hawkins in 1715, because the house sits within a landscaped garden with 18 champion trees, and the current owner has planted more than 30,000 trees.

There are different bays and lawns at Trewithen, which is also an International Camellia Society Garden of Excellence. There's a wildlife garden with flowers for butterflies, and you may also see red squirrels, which live in an enclosure to boost a breeding population to aid wild releases.

Trewithen has developed through history, allowing an exquisite collection of rhododendrons, magnolias, camellias, maples and azaleas to flourish. This is much thanks to plant-hunters, such as E.H. Wilson and George Forrest, who went to exotic locations, bringing seeds back. It is a garden to add to the must-visit list.
Trewithen, Grampound Road, near Truro, Cornwall TR2 4DD. 01726 883647; trewithengardens.co.uk

Images: Shutterstock, Alamy

Shady pathways and sea views make this garden special

LAMORRAN HOUSE GARDENS

On a summer's day, stand under the cupola and look out to sea. This sloped four-acre Italianate-inspired garden is a paradise with a wealth of southern hemisphere and sub-tropical planting, set amongst statues and water features.

Historically, there was no garden here. It was started by the current owners Robert and Maria-Antoinette Dudley-Cooke who, inspired by their travels to the island of Ischia, transformed the area, first planting rhododendrons and azaleas from their Surrey garden. An extraordinary amount of work went into creating this garden, as landscaping on the sloped ground saw temples, ponds and bridges added. Originally, the family travelled to work on the gardens every weekend. It was this dedication that created horticultural bliss here, and the inspiration that keeps it going today.

Visitors can weave amongst the Japanese, Mediterranean and English inspired gardens, while glimpsing the sea. The textures and wealth of foliage that fill the garden is mesmerising, and there's a multitude of tree ferns and palm trees to see. Rest by the edge of the pond to see carp, and appreciate the blue hydrangeas that thrive. The site continues to develop, with a rose garden added in 2014 and a rock garden in 2018. It is a pocket of paradise not to be missed.
Lamorran House Gardens, Upper Castle Road, St Mawes, Cornwall TR2 5BZ. 01326 270800; lamorrangardens.co.uk

GAP/Rebecca Bernstein

TAKING THE PLUNGE

Gregory Holyoake charts the rise of sea bathing

The Sun Court at Scarborough Spa overlooking the beach

Blackpool's famous tower and beach

A SEEMINGLY trivial incident occurred around 1626 when a certain Mrs Farrow, "a gentlewoman of good repute", strolled along the sandy beach at Scarborough, a remote fishing village in North Yorkshire. Here she made a chance discovery that marked the beginning of the English seaside holiday.

She came across a spring of dark russet tincture issuing from the cliffside of the exposed South Bay. Sipping the water, she realised it was chalybeate – spring water containing iron salts – and she recognised immediately its medicinal value.

Until that moment, aristocrats and gentility had made their annual pilgrimage to inland spas where invalids and hypochondriacs regularly sought health cures by drinking sulphur or saline water from natural springs at fashionable towns like Bath, Cheltenham, Harrogate, Buxton, Matlock and Royal Tunbridge Wells. There it was the height of fashion to mingle with the genuinely sick in a hectic social round of balls, banquets, gaming and sight-seeing.

But now the seaside rush was on! Spurred on by the preposterous scribblings of quack doctors who extolled the virtues of not only drinking salt water but bathing in it, the gentry turned their attention to the coast. First by coach, then by

Enjoying the view of Eastbourne's Victorian pier

Antique postcard of bathers on a bathing machine

SKYLARKING.

steamer, hoy and eventually steam railway, health and pleasure seekers of the Victorian and Georgian era flocked to the seaside.

In 1667, Dr Wittie of Hull published his pamphlet where he directed everyone to seaside resorts – in particular to Scarborough. He advanced the theory that immersion in sea water was a cure for everything from deafness to mental disorder.

"It cleanses the stomach, opens the lungs, cures Asthma and Scurvy, purifies the blood, cures Jaunders both yellow and black and the Leprosie," he propounded. "It is a most sovereign Remedy against Hypochondriak, Meloncholy and Windiness . . ."

Dr Richard Russell published his revolutionary treatise, *A Dissertation on the Use of Sea Water*, in 1752, recommending that one unfortunate patient take a course in drinking 24 gallons of sea water. Only hardy folk, however, would have been wise to adhere to the customs attached to the ritual of sea bathing. It was not thought fit, for instance, to open the pores by bathing in hot weather. One bathed in the cold, early morning, preferably in mid-winter.

Diarist Fanny Burney recorded her invigorating bathe when she rose at six for her early morning dip in the English Channel in November 1782. Fanny wrote of the first time she bathed in the sea: "I was terribly frightened, and really thought I should never have recovered from the Plunge – I had not Breath enough to speak for a minute or two, the shock was beyond expression great – but after I got back to the machine, I presently felt myself in a Glow that was delightful."

Jane Austen toured the new seaside resorts of Lyme, Dawlish, Colyton, Teignmouth, Sidmouth, Charmouth, Tenby and Barmouth with her family. She alludes to several beaches in her novels, particularly *Sandition* (published posthumously in 1817) which concerns the emergence of a fashionable resort in Sussex. In late summer 1804, Jane visited Lyme in Dorset, where she caught a fever, and to aid her recovery she took to bathing from a machine attended by her personal "dipper", Molly.

"The bathing was so delightful this morning," Austen recorded, "and I stayed in rather too long."

Royal patronage increased a resort's popularity. In September 1783, George, Prince of Wales, shortly after his 21st birthday, visited the modest Sussex fishing village, Brighthelmstone. There he commissioned a Royal Pavilion with Indian exterior – soaring minarets and onion-shaped domes – and Chinese interior. Young gallants and fashionable ladies followed him in pursuit, turning this remote town into the bustling Brighton we know today.

His father, George III, frequently visited Weymouth and was "dipped" to the accompaniment of a band concealed in a nearby bathing machine. His infant sons, Princes Alfred and Octavius, were dispatched to alleviate their fragile health by bathing at Deal. King George IV's daughter, Princess Charlotte, was "dipped" in the sea at Southend, aged five, in the chilly months of October, November and December.

The invention of the bathing machine, most favoured by female bathers, rapidly increased the popularity of sea bathing. It ensured that it could be enjoyed in a manner "consistent with the most refined delicacy". Little more than wooden huts on wheels, these quaint contraptions transported timid bathers in complete privacy to the water's edge (Queen Victoria's personal bathing machine can still be viewed at Osborne House, Isle of Wight).

Bathing machines had a door at each end and were drawn by horses across the sand or shingle into the sea until the water was level with their steps. These primitive mobile changing rooms can be seen in the engraving >

Railway poster encouraging visitors to Deal

> of Scarborough Bay by John Setterington, which is now in the British Museum.

The person who is generally credited with their invention in around 1750 was a Margate Quaker called Benjamin Beale. He merely improved the existing machines, however, by adding a modesty hood, or "calash", stretched over articulated canvas hoops which managed to screen the shy bather from public gaze as she ventured down the steps into the bleak waters below.

Beale was a glover and breeches maker. He never gained financially from his invention, despite his bathing machines being exported as far away as the East and West Indies. Many of his own machines were destroyed by severe storms and he died penniless in 1775.

An amusing rhyme written in a "feminine hand" was discovered affixed to one of his Margate bathing machines:

*"Though oft have I been
In a bathing machine,
I never discover'd till now,
The wonderful art
Of this little go-cart
Tis vastly convenient, I vow.
A peg for your clothes,
A glass for your nose,
And, shutting the little trap-door.
You are safe from the ken
Of those impudent men
Who wander about on the shore."*

Modesty prevailed at all times, and each individual resort adopted its own strict rules about segregating the sexes.

At Margate, a distance of 60 feet kept men and women apart, while at Blackpool a bell was rung to warn male bathers to disappear, allowing female bathers to take their turn in the briny. Some resorts even insisted on separate beaches for men and women.

Gentlemen at Scarborough were rowed a short way out in hired boats to bathe offshore in privacy, but at Southport the annoyance of prying sailors who attempted to row too near bathing women was overcome by hefty fines. Margate was the first to allow mixed bathing, but not until the beginning of the 20th century.

Inquisitive males who lingered ashore to stare at bathing belles were a constant menace. They were kept at bay by the burly women known as "dippers", whose task was to introduce timid bathers into the delights of sea bathing.

Their methods were indeed unorthodox. After helping the bather to undress, they forcibly plunged their charges repeatedly beneath the chilly waves. To ensure novice swimmers were kept safe, they tied a rope around their waist to rein them if they were deemed to be in danger from being washed away by high waves or heavy swells.

These seaside "dippers" became celebrities. Martha Gunn of Brighton was regarded as a national heroine, being depicted on numerous Toby jugs. Other redoubtable "dippers" were Mrs Nash of Ramsgate, Mrs Knock and Old Jennie of Margate, Widow Ducker of Scarborough, and Mrs Glassock and Mrs Myall, both of Southend, with the latter being hailed for her "particular skill and tenderness". The Prince of Wales commanded his own personal attendant, "Old Smoaker", at Brighton, who, upon his retirement, was awarded a pension.

Men bathed naked as a matter of course until 1863, when bathing drawers, or "calecons", were introduced at Brighton. Next appeared the University swimming costume, named after the one-piece suit designed for swimming contests at colleges and universities. Later came the striped garment of the Edwardian era

Marine Drive and Clock Tower, Margate

Edwardian postcard

before belted trunks appeared in the 1930s. They resembled the original bathing drawers.

Women's bathing costumes were more complicated. Initially, they wore cotton or flannel "cases" tied with string at the neck. These ballooned out in the water, allowing for bathing underneath! Then followed a variety of clumsy, inappropriate costumes. Daring knicker-bockers, sometimes concealed by a weighted knee-length skirt, were accompanied by a calico jacket or blouse buttoned chastely to the neck and gaily decorated with coloured ribbons, collars and sashes. Constructed of cotton or stockinette, these costumes, when wet, clung to the body and were indecent. Corsets were sometimes worn underneath!

Headkerchiefs and mob caps were fashionable accoutrements. In 1880, the first one-piece bathing costume appeared, covering the female form from neck to knee. Made of serge and worn with black or white stockings, and later soft shoes with criss-cross lacing up the leg, such costumes were popular, with modifications, for over 70 years. The bikini made its shattering appearance in the 1950s. Named after Bikini Atoll, where two A-bombs were tested in 1946, its effect on the public was thought to be equally explosive!

Seaside resorts imitated inland spas. They offered innocuous pastimes like plays, dances, lotteries, billiards, card parties and circulating libraries. Assembly rooms hosted social events where a

Holidaymakers on the beach at Margate

master of ceremonies presided over formal gatherings. The aristocracy scanned the list of visitors, regularly printed in local newspapers, to decide whose acquaintance among the new arrivals was considered desirable.

The advance of railways from the 1850s onwards, coupled with the Bank Holiday Act of 1871, ensured that every working person was given at least one day's holiday, which changed the social round drastically, and resorts began to cater for day-trippers.

They found entertainment in concert parties, music halls, pleasure gardens, amusement arcades, penny peep shows, beach fairs, balloon ascents, firework displays, regattas, illuminations, band concerts, skating rinks, donkey rides, Pierrot shows and Punch and Judy. Pleasure piers, enjoyed by promenaders from all walks of life, became popular from the 1880s, when the majority of them were built around our coast. They were a resort's greatest status symbol.

Today, the idea that an excursion to the beach is desirable for health reasons still persists, although a visit to a favourite resort is now undertaken mainly for purposes of pleasure.

And in summer, when the sun shines, a trip to the seaside for the modern family remains the perfect English holiday.

Striped bathing machines at the ready in Hastings

Beach huts at Thorpe Bay, Southend-on-Sea

Images: Shutterstock

SAILING TO A NEW LIFE

The *Empire Windrush* arrived in Britain 75 years ago,
Paul Bloomfield tells the story

ON 22 June 1948, a lilting, unfamiliar accent drifted through the air at Tilbury Docks on the Thames, about 20 miles east of the capital. "London is the place for me," began the smiling crooner, "London, this lovely city!" Over two a cappella verses, the sharply suited singer proclaimed his gladness to know the "mother country".

The author of these optimistic words was already famous in his homeland, Trinidad, as master calypsonian Lord Kitchener. To authorities processing his arrival in England, though, he was Aldwyn Roberts, 26 years old – just one of 802 passengers from the West Indies disembarking the troopship *Empire Windrush*.

These men and women were at the vanguard of a wave of migration from the Caribbean that became known as the "Windrush generation" – some 500,000 Commonwealth citizens who settled in Britain between 1948 and 1971. They believed they were answering a call for help from that "mother country" – but what awaited them wasn't always what they'd anticipated.

In the years following World War II, as British euphoria at the defeat of Nazi Germany subsided, another challenge became evident: gaping holes in the labour force needed to rebuild the battered country. In response, the government attempted to attract workers from overseas, particularly Poles who'd joined the British war effort, and displaced persons from elsewhere in Europe. Then came the British Nationality Act 1948, giving citizens of colonies and the Commonwealth the right to settle in the "homeland".

Even before Lord Kitchener serenaded a Pathé News reporter at Tilbury Docks, a number of West Indians were living and working in Britain. Some were ex-servicemen who'd responded to the call to arms during the war and remained after it was over, with more eastward migration to follow this. The *SS Ormonde* sailed to Liverpool in March 1947, carrying some 100 Jamaicans, many of them ex-servicemen; another 200 landed in Southampton on the *Almanzora* that December. But it was the arrival of the *Windrush* that made national headlines.

Formerly a German cruise liner, the *Monte Rosa*, she had been captured by the British in 1945 and, renamed the *Empire Windrush*, and used as a troopship. She called at Kingston in 1948 en route from Australia, officially to pick up servicemen returning from leave. But in mid-April, an advert appeared in Jamaica's *Daily Gleaner* newspaper, offering a "passenger opportunity" with listed fares starting at £28 10s – a great deal of money, equivalent to the cost of three cows.

Again, many of those who boarded had served in British forces during the war, but the passenger list also names other men, women and children from Jamaica, Bermuda, British Guiana (now Guyana) and Trinidad. There were stowaways, too; when young Jamaican dressmaker Evelyn Wauchope was discovered, her fellow passengers clubbed together to pay for her passage.

Many landing in Tilbury had left behind economies ravaged by war and natural disasters – not least the lethal Jamaica hurricane of 1944 – and planned to earn money in Britain, then return to the Caribbean; others were determined to make a new home. Ostensibly at least, they found a warm reception. "Welcome Home!" boomed the London *Evening Standard* headline on 21 June, greeting "the 400 sons of Empire" aboard the *Windrush*.

Some of the new arrivals had pre-arranged jobs and accommodation, but 236 who had no employment lined up and nowhere to stay were bussed to the deep air-raid shelter beneath Clapham South underground station. There they were provided with a bed and three meals, plus directions to the labour exchange a short walk to the east in Brixton. Many who found work there took lodgings in the area, establishing a community that transformed the then down-at-heel neighbourhood, which had been heavily bombed during the war.

The *Windrush* immigrants were, of course, not the first black Britons. There were Londoners of African heritage during the Roman era, and Queen Elizabeth I had noted the presence of "many Blackamoores". By the mid-20th century, many people of colour lived in Britain, though not in such >

Festivities at Notting Hill Carnival

The famous Brendon Batson

Brixton La

> large numbers that substantial communities had formed. So the arrival of the Windrush generation marked a change – and one that was not welcomed by some in both officialdom and wider British society.

Even before the *Windrush* departed Kingston, British Prime Minster Clement Attlee had looked into having the ship diverted so that West Indians on board could be sent to work on groundnut farms in East Africa instead of coming to England. And after its arrival, 11 Labour MPs wrote to Attlee requesting that the "influx" be stemmed. In fact, immigration numbers from the Caribbean remained modest following the arrival of the *Windrush*. By 1950, only a few thousand West Indians

had arrived in Britain. But following further devastation wreaked on Jamaica by Hurricane Charlie in 1951, and a tightening of US immigration policy the next year, more Commonwealth citizens crossed the Atlantic.

And during the 1950s and early 1960s, recruitment campaigns by major employers such as London Transport, British Rail, the NHS and hospitality industry bodies boosted arrivals. Numbers of British residents born in the West Indies increased from about 15,000 in 1951 to an estimated 172,000 in 1961. The following year, though, the Commonwealth Immigrants Act 1962 introduced stringent restrictions on immigration, substantially reducing the number of people coming to Britain from

the West Indies.

Such resistance to immigration of people of colour reflected antipathy from some employers, shopkeepers and owners of homes to rent, who in 1948 placed signs in their windows saying "No Blacks". In stark contrast to the optimistic *London is the Place for Me*, in Lord Kitchener's later song *If You're Brown* he recalls being told by white people that "you can't stick around". Over the following decade, such prejudice fomented tensions that erupted into violence in Notting Hill and Nottingham in 1958.

Over time, overt racism has been tackled in employment, sport and wider society. Still, the challenges faced by the Windrush generation continued for many decades. The "hostile environment" policy adopted by the UK Home Office from 2012 to deter undocumented migrants resulted in deportation, detainment or the loss of homes, jobs or access to medical care for many who arrived in Britain from the West Indies before 1973 – some as children, spending their entire adult lives in the UK.

As Commonwealth citizens, at the time of their arrival most had not needed documentation on entry confirming a long-term right to remain. But after Caribbean countries gained independence, and legislation limited the rights of Commonwealth citizens to come

Demonstrations in London on Windrush Day, which remembers the arrival of the troopship

ge, where many immigrants found work

Caribbean food on offer at Camden Market

to the UK, that became a problem. The onus fell on those affected to prove their long-term residence, requiring documentation that in many cases had never existed or had long since been lost or destroyed – including landing cards collected on arrival. The fallout from the "Windrush scandal" continued into 2022 as compensation cases dragged on.

Despite such challenges, and ongoing discrimination from some quarters, the Caribbean community has successfully established itself and made its mark on the British economy, culture and society. The NHS has depended heavily on the many doctors, nurses and other staff from Commonwealth and other countries. The sports grounds of Britain have been graced by countless talented players and athletes born in the region or with Caribbean heritage – to give just one example, Brendon Batson, from Grenada via Trinidad, one of the groundbreaking "Three Degrees" lit up football stadia during the 1970s and early '80s.

In 1959, Trinidadian-born activist Claudia Jones organised a small-scale Caribbean carnival at St Pancras Town Hall; also involved was Jamaican Sam King, who had arrived aboard the *Windrush* and later became the first black Mayor of Southwark. The appetite for such events was huge, and from the mid-1960s

street festivals evolved into the now-famous Notting Hill Carnival celebrating Caribbean culture, music, food and dance across three days in August.

Indeed, all kinds of music in Britain have drawn on sounds and styles brought here by Caribbean migrants, from the calypso music sung by "Kitch" and fellow "Trinis" aboard the *Windrush* to Jamaican reggae and dub, feeding into punk, ska, trip hop, grime and many other genres. Writers also made their mark, notably luminaries such as Trinidadian-

born author VS Naipaul, who came to England in 1950, and Jamaican-born playwright Alfred Fagon, who initially worked for British Rail after arriving in 1955.

This island has experienced many waves of migration, from the arrival of Neolithic farmers eight millennia ago through influxes of Romans, Angles and Saxons, Danes and Normans, and many more over the centuries. The arrival of *Empire Windrush* 75 years ago marked another watershed moment in the evolution of today's multicultural Britain.

West Indian immigrants arrive at London Victoria Station, 1960

The Colours
of Autumn

by Robert B. Thomas

The colours of autumn
Are here for a visit.
Red, yellow and brown,
They are so exquisite.

I walk through those leaves
That are now on the ground,
So crunchy, so crispy,
A true autumn sound.

But now I must rake them,
A real autumn duty,
To prepare for the snow
And all of its beauty.

Roundhay Park in West Yorkshire

Image: Shutterstock

SUMMER TO AUTUMN

Events of the season, luxury train travel, how our towns and villages get their names, plus test your knowledge of politics   >

SUMMER TO AUTUMN

Katherine Sorrell on gooseberries, garlic, the first Paralympics, Concorde in the air and the birth of the NHS

JULY 2023

Britain's Katherine Comley in the Rome Paralympics, 1960

75 YEARS OF THE PARALYMPIC MOVEMENT

The spinal injuries centre at Stoke Mandeville Hospital opened in 1944, initially treating servicemen injured in the war. Sport was used for rehabilitation, which evolved into competition. On 29 July 1948, the day of the opening ceremony of the London 1948 Olympics, centre director Dr Ludwig Guttmann organised a competition for 16 wheelchair athletes, which he named the Stoke Mandeville Games. It was the start of the Paralympic movement.

COWES WEEK

The oldest, largest annual sailing regatta in the world is a key feature in the sporting calendar, this year starting on 29 July. The Isle of Wight event stages up to 40 daily races for around 750 boats, alongside plenty of social activities. The fireworks take place on the final Friday. **cowesweek.co.uk**

WORLD SNAIL RACING CHAMPIONSHIPS

They say that Congham is to snails what Newmarket is to horses. The championships, usually on the third Saturday of July, are part of the village fete in Congham, Norfolk, and all comers are welcome. Simply select your garden snail and turn up. Ready, set . . . slow! **snailracing.net**

HENLEY ROYAL REGATTA

It's both an elite sporting event and a social highlight, set in picturesque Henley-on-Thames and usually ending on the first weekend in July. An international rowing regatta with more than 300 races, from single sculls to eights, it features Olympians and emerging stars from around the world. **hrr.co.uk**

Buying plants at Hampton Court

RHS HAMPTON COURT PALACE GARDEN FESTIVAL

It's the world's largest flower show set against the impressive backdrop of Hampton Court, one of the UK's most famous palaces. Explore the show gardens, take part in a workshop, shop for your outside space, enjoy a picnic or catch an expert talk. Be inspired. **rhs.org.uk**

HAPPY 75TH BIRTHDAY TO THE NHS

On 5 July 1948, when health minister Nye Bevan visited Park Hospital, Manchester (now Trafford General), the National Health Service was incorporated. Doctors, nurses, pharmacists, opticians, dentists and hospitals became one UK-wide institution, funded from taxation and free at the point of use. Bevan's creation made history as the first health system in any Western society to offer free medical care for all.

Nye Bevan visits Park Hospital

BUXTON INTERNATIONAL FESTIVAL

Buxton's annual festival, now running for more than 40 years, celebrates opera, music and literature in the heart of the Peak District. It is one of Europe's most impressive (yet friendly) culture festivals. The hills are alive with the sound of . . . opera!
buxtonfestival.co.uk

BBC PROMS

The biggest classical music festival in the world is held at London's Royal Albert Hall. Its aim is to bring the finest classical music to as many people as possible. The programme includes classical favourites, contemporary world premieres and family concerts, with the "Last Night" usually on the second Saturday in September.
bbc.co.uk/proms

Ooh arrrrr. Pirates in Hastings

HASTINGS PIRATE DAY(S)

Why are pirates called pirates? Just because they arrrrr! The world capital of pirates is, believe it or not, the East Sussex seaside town of Hastings, which has held the Guinness World Record for the most pirates in one place since 2012 (14,231), despite attempts to topple it by Penzance and others. This much-loved annual community festival, in its 14th year, includes live music, storytelling and pirate-themed activities. Get out your best striped top and parrot and join in the fun. **hastingspirateday.org**

SEAFEAST: THE DORSET SEAFOOD FESTIVAL

Celebrating Dorset's links with the sea and fishing, the UK's largest free seafood festival takes place around Weymouth's historic Old Harbour. Expect live music, demonstrations from leading chefs and fabulous street food.
dorsetseafood.co.uk

GREAT YORKSHIRE SHOW

Now a four-day event, this is one of the biggest agricultural shows in the English calendar, showcasing the best of British farming, food and the countryside at the Great Yorkshire Showground in Harrogate.
greatyorkshireshow. co.uk

SWAN UPPING

The annual census of swans on the Thames is an important element of wildlife conservation. In July, a flotilla of traditional Thames rowing skiffs, manned by Swan "Uppers" spend five days rowing up the river to check the swans' health. **royal.uk/swans**

ROYAL INTERNATIONAL AIR TATTOO

Reputed to be the biggest military airshow in the world, held at RAF Fairford, Gloucestershire, the Air Tattoo features modern and classic aircraft, and static and flying exhibits from around the world – with more than seven hours of spectacular flying each day.
airtattoo.com

>

60TH ANNIVERSARY OF THE GREAT TRAIN ROBBERY

It was late on 8 August 1963. The Glasgow to London Royal Mail train, carrying £2.6 million, mostly in used bank notes, was stopped by 15 masked robbers who coshed the driver, uncoupled the engine and the first two carriages, and drove off with the cash.

They unloaded 120 mail sacks on to Land Rovers, then hid in a nearby farmhouse, playing Monopoly using real money.

A huge police operation resulted – eventually – in every gang member being arrested and tried.

Ronnie Biggs escaped from Wandsworth Prison in a furniture van and fled to Brazil (via Paris, for plastic surgery on his face), but was finally re-arrested, returning to the UK in 2001.

He served a further eight years before being released because of poor health.

A bag of cash from the robbery

BRISTOL INTERNATIONAL BALLOON FIESTA

The incredible sight of hundreds of hot-air balloons filling the skies above Bristol is surely one not to be missed. Europe's largest annual balloon meeting attracts participants from across the globe, with mass ascents and night-time illuminations in time to music, plus ground-level stalls, fairground rides and plenty of entertainment. Now's the time to fulfil that lifetime ambition to book a ride in the sky . . . **bristolballoonfiesta.co.uk**

Flying high

FAVERSHAM HOP FESTIVAL

Believed to have been introduced to Britain by the Romans, hops were first brewed in England in the 15th century, with Kent becoming a centre for hop growing, reaching a peak in the late 19th century. One of the largest free street festivals in the South East, Faversham Hop Festival is a family-friendly affair, attracting tens of thousands each year. Enjoy a parade, performances and traditional dancing, live music, market stalls, street food, a funfair, puppet shows, shire horses and tours of Shepherd Neame, Britain's oldest brewers. **favershamhopfestival.org**

Garlic of every description

ISLE OF WIGHT GARLIC FESTIVAL

Every year since 1983 the Isle of Wight Garlic Festival has been held on the third weekend in August just outside Newchurch. At the heart of the festival, available to eat, drink and buy au naturel, is the garlic bulb, grown at the nearby garlic farm. There's also live music and entertainment, a theatre kitchen, children's activities and market stalls, attracting young and old alike. **garlicfestival.co.uk**

THE INTERNATIONAL GILBERT AND SULLIVAN FESTIVAL

This celebration of the works of the Victorian operatic duo brings together a mix of professional and leading amateur groups performing in both Buxton and Harrogate, plus fringe events, talks and more. **gsfestivals.org**

EGTON BRIDGE GOOSEBERRY SHOW

The oldest gooseberry show in the country was established at Egton Bridge, North Yorkshire, back in 1800. Each year, on the first Tuesday in August, members of the village's Old Gooseberry Society enter their prize fruit, the heaviest to be determined by a precise apothecary scale. **egtongooseberryshow.org.uk**

CHILLI FESTIVALS

Established in 2006, the popular Chilli Festival attracts thousands of visitors to the gardens of the historic Benington Lordship house, Hertfordshire, over three days around the August bank holiday. At least 60 pitches from the nation's best known chilli traders offer everything, including chutneys, sauces, pickles, seeds, cheese and chocolate – and there's also great food and drink, a range of entertainment and a chilli-eating competition. Don't miss the stunning gardens, too, which are rarely open to the public.

Chilli festivals take place around England, many during the summer. Chilli Fest at Waddesdon Manor gathers local artisan producers and independent traders alongside live music, children's activities and the chance to walk around the gardens, while the Cheese and Chilli Festival takes place at four locations in the south of England: Christchurch, Winchester, Swindon and Guildford. Many regular, smaller, street chilli

Now's the time to visit a chilli festival

fiestas are organised in a number of towns by Chilli Fest UK.
**beningtonlordship.co.uk/chilli-festival;
waddesdon.org.uk/whats-on/chilli-festival;
cheeseandchillifestival.com;
readingchillifest.co.uk;
em-chillifest.com; chillifestuk.net**

THE BRITISH FIREWORK CHAMPIONSHIPS

Each year six professional firework display companies are selected by draw to put on a 10-minute show for this spectacular two-night competition. Plymouth's harbour and Sound is the ideal venue for a large-scale pyrotechnical battle, plus there's entertainment on the Hoe with a funfair, live music and food and drink. The displays are designed to be seen from Citadel and the Hoe – but be sure to arrive early for a good spot.
britishfireworks.co.uk

Lytham goes back to the 1940s

ARUNDEL FESTIVAL OF THE ARTS

This free community event in Arundel, West Sussex, is one of the largest multi-arts festivals in the South, taking place over 10 days around the August bank holiday each year and featuring an art gallery trail, music, drama, street entertainment, comedy, cabaret and more.
arundelfestival.co.uk

LYTHAM 1940S WARTIME WEEKEND

Lytham St Annes' popular event attracts visitors to Lancashire from all over the country. Roll back the decades and immerse yourself in the spirit of the wartime era with singing, dancing, big bands, talks, historic vehicles and vintage traders. Daytime entertainment in the main marquee is free. **discoverfylde.co.uk/lytham1940s**

Spectacular Kynren

KYNREN: AN EPIC TALE OF ENGLAND

Held at Flatts Farm in Bishop Auckland, Durham, every Saturday in the summer, this award-winning open-air spectacular employs a cast of 1,500 to reveal the history, myth and legend of England over 2,000 years. A new daytime attraction includes a horse stunt show and a range of immersive experiences, followed by a range of dining options and the evening live-action show itself.
11arches.com/kynren

>

50TH ANNIVERSARY OF CONCORDE'S FIRST ATLANTIC CROSSING

It was the first supersonic, passenger-carrying commercial aeroplane. Concorde, a joint venture between Britain and France, made its first non-stop crossing of the Atlantic in the record-breaking time of three hours and 32 minutes on 26 September 1973.

Sleek and fast: Concorde

THE JOHN MOORES PAINTING PRIZE

First held in 1957, the John Moores Painting Prize is the country's best-known painting biennale, its roll-call of past winners reading like a who's who of British painting over the past 50 years. The competition aims to bring together the best in contemporary British painting. The exhibition of this year's winners opens in September 2023 at Liverpool's highly esteemed Walker Art Gallery. **liverpoolmuseums.org. uk/jmpp/john-moores-painting-prize**

LUDLOW FOOD FESTIVAL

Ludlow in Shropshire has been described as the UK's second gourmet capital, and its annual three-day food festival involves talks, celebrity chef demos and tastings, plus feasts, masterclasses, workshops and more, with over 100 local food and drink producers and suppliers, all held inside the grounds of Ludlow Castle. **ludlowfoodfestival.co.uk**

HERITAGE OPEN DAYS

See hidden places and try out new experiences in England's largest festival of history, architecture and culture. Every year in September, places across the country throw open their doors, allowing you to see inside historic homes, museum archives, castles, boats, gardens and all sorts of fascinating buildings, many of which are usually closed to the public. Thousands of events take place across the nation, all of them free. **heritageopendays.org.uk**

EGREMONT CRAB FAIR

Named for crab apples as opposed to crustaceans, this fair was established in picturesque Egremont, Cumbria, in 1267, making it one of the oldest in the world. Traditional events combine with modern attractions, starting on the Friday night with a free concert in Main Street. The highlight of Saturday is a parade in which apples are thrown from a cart. There's local food and craft, ferret shows, equestrian events and more, including the World Gurning Championships, at 6pm in the Falcon Pub. **egremontcrabfair.com**

MATLOCK BATH ILLUMINATIONS

First held in 1897 to celebrate Queen Victoria's Diamond Jubilee, the Matlock Bath Illuminations is a unique floating parade that now takes place every year on weekend evenings in September and October. The display of themed models is decorated with thousands of lights, mounted on rowing boats to be paraded along the River Derwent. As darkness falls, the brightly lit models appear to glide along the water by themselves. Expect a carnival atmosphere! **derbyshiredales.gov.uk/things-to-do/whats-on/ matlock-bath-illuminations**

WIDECOMBE FAIR

Run entirely by volunteers to raise money for local good causes, as well as providing an opportunity for farmers to compare the size of their tractors, Widecombe Fair takes place on the second Tuesday of September each year in Dartmoor, Devon, and attracts visitors from far and wide. It's the epitome of a charming country fair, with everything from tug o' war to bale tossing, a dog and duck display to the ever-popular terrier race. **widecombefair.com**

ABBOTS BROMLEY HORN DANCE

Wakes Monday is the first Monday following the first Sunday after 4 September, and also the date for an unusual rural ritual held in Abbots Bromley, Staffordshire, each year. First performed in 1226, it is England's oldest danced tradition, and consists of a 12-strong team of men, including six Deer-men (wearing horns), a Fool, Hobby Horse, Bowman and Maid Marian, who dance a course of about 10 miles through the village and farms and pubs, accompanied by a melodeon. The horns are 1,000-year-old reindeer antlers, possibly brought to England by Vikings. **abbotsbromley.com**

The Deer-men at work

ALDEBURGH FOOD AND DRINK FESTIVAL

This jam-packed weekend of food adventures at the Snape Maltings arts complex in Aldeburgh celebrates the abundance, quality and variety of Suffolk's food and drink, and includes tastings and demonstrations, workshops, discussions and, of course, shopping opportunities with more than 100 local producers. Two weeks of fringe events take place across Suffolk. **aldeburghfoodanddrink.co.uk**

Snape, site of the food festival

PEARLY KINGS AND QUEENS HARVEST FESTIVAL

Celebrate the harvest with the Pearly Kings and Queens of London, who will be decked out in their traditional finery of dark suits with bright pearl buttons. It's the biggest event in the Pearly calendar, and there's traditional entertainment with maypole dancing and marching bands in front of the Guildhall, before a parade through the streets to St Mary Le Bow Church for a service of thanksgiving. **pearlysociety.co.uk**

The Pearlies meet the Chelsea Pensioners

SHEEP DRIVE AND LIVERY FAIR

In medieval times, farmers drove their sheep across London Bridge into the City of London to sell them at market, with Freemen of the City excused the bridge toll.

This practice had all but died out by the early 20th century, but in 2013 the Worshipful Company of Woolmen arranged for Freemen of the City and their guests to officially "drive" sheep across the Thames, once again upholding the tradition of Freemen's rights. The event was so successful that it has continued ever since, although it now takes place on Southwark Bridge. **sheepdrive.london**

JANE AUSTEN FESTIVAL

The Regency era comes to life with this annual celebration of all things Austen, featuring more than 80 events from walks, talks and discussions to dances, promenades and performances. **janeausten festivalbath.co.uk**

LONDON DESIGN FESTIVAL

Celebrating and promoting London as the design capital of the world, this nine-day festival features events, exhibitions and installations across the city, and this year reaches the grand old age of 21. From Brompton to Mayfair, in world-famous museums and intimate shops and studios, designers of all kinds present new ideas and new products, and explore new ways of thinking through exhibitions, tours, workshops, talks, discussions and more. While showcasing design's joyous side, the programme also aims to introduce innovations that have the capacity to shape our society. Landmark public installations are a key feature, as are Design Districts, comprising clusters of events within a short walk of each other. It's huge! **londondesignfestival.com**

Giant chess at the London Design Festival

Images Shutterstock, Alamy

CORFE CASTLE, DORSET

This fairy-tale-like ruin
was one of England's
first stone castles, says
Chris Franks

Corfe Castle perched on its hilltop

THERE is something profoundly mysterious about Corfe Castle. The moment you see this dreamy ruin near Wareham on the Dorset coast, your mind starts to roam. It is both beguiling and intriguing at the same time and it seems to remind you of something . . . but you don't know what.

You enter across a bridge, flanked by the stunted remains of two turrets. From the outer bailey, you gaze up at the south-west gatehouse, the strata of the great ditch like giant stairs. It's all strangely familiar and you are drawn upward, to the craggy pinnacle of the keep, as if there you will find the answer.

Corfe Castle's enigmatic aura is due partly to its hilltop position. It's like something out of a fairy tale. Yet despite what many believe, hilltop castles weren't common. The best places to build castles were by strategically important points, such as roads or river crossings, which were often lower down. The site for Corfe was chosen to guard an important pass through the Purbeck Hills.

Corfe was one of England's first castles built in stone. The earliest parts were laid during the reign of William the Conqueror. The spectacular 80-foot keep was constructed by Henry I in the early 1100s. Standing on top of a 180-foot hill, it dominated the landscape for miles.

Most of the other stonework was built by King John and his son, Henry III, over the first half of the 13th century.

Like many medieval fortresses, Corfe was already past its best by the 17th century, but was forced into conflict during the English Civil War. By then, it was owned by Sir John Bankes, Attorney General to Charles I and a staunch Royalist. While he was away fighting with the king, his wife Lady Mary held the castle with a small garrison against two Parliamentarian sieges. In the first, she was victorious, bravely resisting for six weeks before being relieved, but in the second, she was betrayed by one of her own commanders. The castle was taken and by order of Parliament, was demolished in 1646.

Standing so tall, its destruction was particularly violent, sending huge fragments avalanching down the hillside and leaving the wild, shattered appearance it has today. From a distance, it looks more like a mountain now.

Your journey takes you up through the west bailey and inner ward, as the afternoon light fades and the shadows grow cold. It ends at the top of the hill, among the slender wafers of keep, the empty doorways hanging in space and the ten-foot-thick jagged blocks racked at 45 degrees. There, you linger, watching the sunset, still wondering what it is this place reminds you of. But you never find it.

You know it's something beautiful and true, though, and in the end that's all that matters.

Some mysteries are best left unsolved.

Images: Alamy

The lesser-known Jerusalem

Alnmouth, the "settlement on the mouth of the Aln"

WHAT'S IN A
Place Name?

Eleanor Doughty on unusual place names
across England and where they derive from

JUST off the A46 near Lincoln, in the midst of lush arable land dotted with cyclists, is a small, innocuous sign. It reads "Jerusalem". The visitor to this part of the country is not seeing things: there really is a Jerusalem in Lincolnshire. It is little more than a winding road to the next village, lined with houses and farm buildings, but it still provokes a smile from locals. Its name derives from the 15th-century pilgrimages taken to the more famous Jerusalem, explains historian Simon Sebag Montefiore in his book *Jerusalem: The Biography*. Since the Jerusalem of biblical prominence was a little too far-flung for the average medieval family, Lincolnshire's own sprung up, just six miles from the gargantuan Lincoln Cathedral.

Jerusalem is not the only place name in the great county of Lincolnshire that makes one do a double-take. The village of New York sits within the parish of Wildmore, itself within Wildmore Fen, which was one of the last to be drained in 1802. New York doesn't appear on any maps before 1800, and it is thought that the navvies who dug the drains came from York – hence calling the surrounding area New York. Today, the village is one in miniature: a former Methodist church-cum-family-home sits on its crossroads, while further down the road is a lecture hall.

Wonderfully, England is full of unusual place names, says Dr John Baker, lecturer at the University of Nottingham and part of its Institute of Name Studies. "Names like New York and Jerusalem often started as minor names within a parish, and were names given to, for example, a field that was furthest away from the centre of

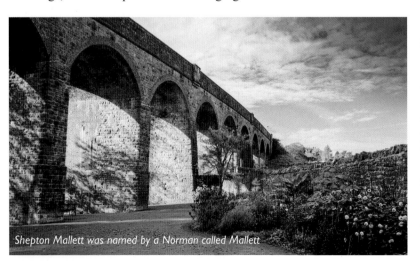

Shepton Mallett was named by a Norman called Mallett

Westward Ho! is the only place name in Britain with an exclamation mark

Hertfordshire's Cow Roast is named after a local pub

the parish." These names were a way of saying that something was a long way off.

Other names arose in different contexts. As Dr Baker points out, there are a number of villages and small towns originally named after pubs. Cow Roast in Hertfordshire is one, as is Craven Arms in Shropshire. "Place names are generally given by local people naming things in ways which are meaningful to them. Naming a village after the famous pub there is not a bad idea."

However, not all names can be easily explained. "We can't always work out why names came about," admits Dr Baker. "The general trends and patterns of naming go back a long way – naming places after individuals or significant features in the landscape is what people have been doing for thousands of years."

Some, though, are easy to decipher. "The Shepton of Shepton Mallett is pure and simply 'Sheep Town', but it was given to a Norman called Mallett who stuck his name on the end of it," explains Caroline Taggart, author of *The Book of English Place Names*. "Almost anywhere you go in the country where you get a two-word name like that, that's the answer." Skipton, says Taggart, is similar: "'Skip' is the Norse for 'sheep', 'ton' is for 'town'."

The village of Alnmouth and the town of Alnwick, on the picturesque east coast in Northumberland, both derive from the River Aln, the former being the "settlement on the mouth of the Aln", and the latter a "dwelling or farm on the River Aln," as AD Mills's *Dictionary of British Place Names* has it.

The North Yorkshire village of Ellingstring is less clear, but is defined by Mills as being the "water-course at the place where eels are caught". In Worcestershire the village of Mamble is "probably a derivative of Celtic mamm [meaning] 'breast-like hill'", while the village of Snailwell in Cambridgeshire is, the dictionary states, from "spring or stream infested with snails".

Rather satisfyingly, the Earl of Portsmouth has an almost cartoonish surname – Wallop. The name was first mentioned in the Domesday Book in 1086, as "Wallope". Mills suggests that the name means "possibly 'valley with a spring or stream'." The Portsmouths' line can be traced back to, at least, Richard Wallop, MP for Hampshire in the early 14th century. It isn't just a surname, but the name of three villages in the Test Valley in Hampshire, The Wallops: Nether, Over, and Middle Wallop.

The task of reading through any dictionary of place names is one that gives much joy; on every page appears something to raise a smile. Indeed, the Yorkshire Wolds village of Wetwang might elicit a snigger. That it sits at a crossroads probably explains how it got its name: this was likely "Vertvanger" originally, the Viking word for "meeting place". Tangmere, in West Sussex, was a key location for Battle of Britain pilots during World War II. Its name, peculiarly, is said to mean "tongs-shaped pool", or as one resident told me, "a serpent's tongue next to a pool".

Other names, however, have more obvious origins. The seaside village of Westward Ho! in Devon – the only place name in Britain that contains an exclamation mark – was inspired by the author Charles Kingsley. When his novel of the same name was published in 1855, a hotel called the Westward Ho!-tel was opened to encourage tourists to the area, and Victorian seaside-goers flocked to its beaches. As such, Westward Ho! was very much created, rather than having evolved. Now, it is a popular surfing spot, with a rock sea pool for swimming.

Apparently peculiar and out-of-place place names are not unique to the British Isles. Look across a world map and many familiar names appear – such as on the East Coast of America, where in the 50 miles between Rutland, Massachusetts and the city of Boston, one encounters Shrewsbury, Marlborough, and Cambridge alone.

Zimbabwe was, until 1980, >

DUKES AND SANDWICHES

The Duke of Devonshire

The Duke of Devonshire also has an unusual name, all things considered. The majority of the Duke's lands, and those owned by his family the Cavendishes, are in Derbyshire. Given this, Masters writes, "the story got about that a scribe had made a mistake, and that 'Devonshire' was written on the patent in error. In fact the patent of 1618 quite clearly says 'Comes Devon' [comes means 'earl'] and that of 1694 equally clearly says 'Dux Devon' . . . the 'shire' was added to the end by common consent to avoid confusion with the other earldom of Devon." The holder of this title does indeed live in Devon, at Powderham Castle.

The Duke of Wellington

The Waterloo hero Arthur Wellesley, future Duke of Wellington, had his title chosen for him by his brother William, who had ransacked the peerage for ideas, and then examined the map, as Brian Masters explains in his 1975 book *The Dukes*. There was a place in Somerset called Welleslie, and not far from this, a town called Wellington. "I trust that you will not think there is anything unpleasant or trifling in the name of Wellington," wrote William to his brother. "I think you have chosen most fortunately," said Arthur, who went on to be the Duke of Wellington. Now, there are many other Wellingtons around: the boot, the London army barracks, and a giant sequoia tree, initially named Wellington gigantea, native to California – plus at least 50 pubs.

The Duke of Wellington

The Earl of Sandwich

The humble sandwich, familiar to us all, is said to take its name from an unusual source. When in 1762 John Montagu, 4th Earl of Sandwich, was playing cards one evening, he pioneered what we now know as the sandwich – two slices of bread with, in Lord Sandwich's case, a piece of roast beef between them – as it was something he could hold in one hand and keep playing cards.

> called Rhodesia; in my main line of work interviewing aristocratic men in their 90s, I often find myself talking about Rhodesia, and its capital Harare, formerly Salisbury, which was renamed in 1982. Rhodesia itself was named by the politician and colonialist Cecil Rhodes, and Salisbury after the UK Prime Minister Lord Salisbury upon its foundation in 1890 by Rhodes's forces.

Other countries retain similar throwbacks. There are 35 other places in the world beyond the south-western English city called Bristol – in Canada, Costa Rica, Jamaica, Peru, Barbados, and the United States, where there are several. In Australia, there is a Chipping Norton, like the fashionable Oxfordshire counterpart, and a Saddleworth, like the moor in the Peak District National Park. Wellington is the capital of New Zealand, and took its name in 1840 from the 1st Duke of Wellington; equally, in Wiltshire, there is a village called New Zealand, thought to be named for Sir John Dickson-Poynder, the early 20th-century MP for Chippenham, who served as Governor of New Zealand from 1910 to 1912.

We may chuckle at some of these names, but they are key to our sense of self. "English place names are as much part of England's cultural heritage as the English language from which they spring," writes Mills. My favourite has to be the village of Pity Me, near Durham. Many tales of its meaning abound, but the best one relates to monks escaping from Lindisfarne after a Viking raid, carrying Saint Cuthbert's coffin with them.

Near the end of their journey, they accidentally dropped the coffin, and the saint's corpse cried out, "Pity me!"

Skipton, or "Sheep Town"

THE FIRST GREAT SEX SCANDAL

Andrew Shaw recalls the Profumo affair which happened 60 years ago

HELPED by a scintillating combination of sex and spies, the Profumo affair was the scandal that got post-war Brits talking about sex, brought down an up-and-coming minister and helped topple a government. Even French President Charles de Gaulle was fascinated, once remarking to an aide, "That'll teach the English for trying to behave like Frenchmen." Almost no one came out untarnished, from the model who survived it to the scapegoat who didn't.

But what was it about this particular scandal that stuck with us, even 60 years later? Profumo was hardly the first politician caught sleeping with someone they shouldn't have been. In that era alone, you can look to Labour leader Hugh Gaitskell and Labour MP Roy Jenkins, not to mention Tory MP Robert Boothby, who spent well over 30 years sleeping with Prime Minister Harold Macmillan's wife. Crucially, though, these affairs were only common knowledge among the elite. Historian Richard Davenport-

The Profumo affair was the subject of the film Scandal with Ian Mckellen and Joanne Whalley-Kilmer

Christine Keeler on her release from prison

Images: Shutterstock, Alamy

Hines argued that Profumo changed that. Before he was exposed, "newspapers protected politicians who were detected in adultery, or caught in the bushes with guardsmen. After 1963, Fleet Street's emetic brew of guilty joys, false tears, nasty surprises and dirty surmises seemed limitless".

It was a tale of two classes. On one side, there was John "Jack" Profumo, son of a Baron and educated at Oxford. He entered the House of Commons at just 25, and as the 1960s began with him as Secretary for War, many thought of him as the future Foreign Secretary.

On the other side was Christine Keeler. Her father abandoned the family when she was five years old, forcing them to move into a house converted from two railway carriages, where she spent her childhood in poverty and fear. Leaving school with no qualifications and no steady income, she quickly became pregnant with a boy she would name Peter, but had to give birth in

secret at home due to her mother's embarrassment. Born prematurely, Peter didn't live a week.

"I was just seventeen," Keeler later wrote. "I did not have many illusions left. The ones that did remain were soon to vanish."

But if Christine had one thing in her favour as a young woman, it was her astonishing beauty. This, coupled with the burning desire to leave the village she despised, led her to London, where she ended up working as a topless showgirl at Murray's Cabaret Club for £8.50 a week. Her story might have ended there if not for Dr Stephen Ward.

Ward had one foot in elite circles due to his successful osteopath business, and over the years, his client list featured the likes of Elizabeth Taylor, Frank Sinatra and Sophia Loren, as well as a raft of politicians such as Winston Churchill and Harold Wilson. When he wasn't healing the bodies of stars and statesmen, he was throwing wild parties where comely young women rubbed shoulders with rich, older men.   >

Dr Stephen Ward leaving the Old Bailey

Mandy Rice-Davies and Christine Keeler, two principal witnesses in Ward's trial

> A regular mainstay of these get-togethers was close friend Yevgeny Ivanov, naval attaché to the Soviet Embassy and secretly a Russian spy. MI5, the UK's security intelligence agency, were aware but believed he could be persuaded to cross over, so started working with Ward in an attempt to convince the Russian.

A chance encounter at Murray's drew Ward and Keeler together. She found herself enraptured by his company, while he enjoyed having a protégée he could show off at his parties. Although she soon moved into his flat, they never slept together, and Keeler described their relationship as "like brother and sister".

For a while, she lived from one party to the next, but it couldn't last forever, and the beginning of the end can be traced to the weekend of 8 July, 1961.

Ward was throwing one of his usual soirées alongside Keeler at the cottage he rented in the grounds of Cliveden House. Meanwhile, the mansion's owner, the 3rd Viscount Astor, was hosting just up the road at the main house. Among the storied elite were Profumo and his wife. By day, the two parties stayed apart, but as the sun started to dip and anticipation for the evening rose, the groups came together at the swimming pool.

Emerging from a naked dip, with just a skimpy towel wrapped around her, Keeler was introduced to Profumo. The next day, the two parties reconvened once again.

Profumo's lust for Keeler was obvious, with one witness stating he "couldn't take his eyes off her, despite the sobering presence of his wife". Their affair began soon after.

The first inkling that something was wrong occurred on 9 August, when Profumo received a call from the most senior civil servant in the land, Cabinet Secretary Sir Norman Brook. In the aftermath of the Cliveden pool party, Ward had told his MI5 handler Woods all about Profumo's interest in the girl. Woods had passed the information on to the agency's director-general, who had in turn alerted Brook.

He warned Profumo to be careful around Ward and his circle, as MI5 didn't feel confident in the osteopath's pro-Soviet views. Keeler didn't come up, but the minister was still spooked, and later that day wrote her a letter stating he wouldn't be able to meet for a while.

If the affair didn't end there, it fizzled out towards the end of the year. By 1962, it was almost like nothing had ever happened. Except for one key detail: Keeler had been having an affair with Ivanov while seeing Profumo. At the height of the Cold War, the British Secretary of War had been playing six degrees of separation with Stalin.

Rumours of what had happened occasionally drifted down Fleet Street, but this was an era where politicians' private lives were actually private, even in the tabloids. An unrelated incident in

December may have been the only reason the scandal was unearthed when it was.

Aside from her fling with the War Secretary, Keeler had been seeing a jazz promoter called Johnny Edgecombe, but ended things when he became violent and possessive. Taking this badly, he turned up at Ward's flat and demanded to be let in. When he wasn't, he took out a gun and fired at the door. His subsequent arrest finally gave the media a reason to start digging into Keeler.

Making matters worse, Keeler began to talk. One night, she spilled the details to a former MP, John Lewis, who not only wanted rid of the Tories in Downing Street, but held a massive grudge against Ward after the osteopath had introduced his girlfriend to the woman she soon ran away with.

The public still had no clue, but in more elite circles the affair was quickly becoming well-known enough for Keeler to go to the press with her story, but with no luck. Even the Soviets could sense things weren't right and recalled Ivanov in late January 1963.

Edgecombe's trial on 14 March kicked things up a notch. Keeler was a key witness but unbeknownst to the court and media, she'd gone to Spain, leading newspapers to hint at Profumo's involvement with carefully placed front page photographs and headlines.

Although every paper in the country knew of the rumours, Labour MP George Wigg commented that they were "willing

Spring Cottage, Cliveden, was where Christine Keeler met John Profumo

John Profumo and wife Valerie Hobson

to wound but afraid to strike".

A week later, Wigg used parliamentary privilege to bring the matter to the House. The fact that Labour were now getting involved with the rumours worried the Tories even more than the press.

On 22 March Profumo stood in front of Parliament and stated there had been "no impropriety whatsoever in my acquaintanceship with Miss Keeler".

At first, Keeler and Ward supported Profumo's statement, despite the former trying to sell her story to every newspaper available. Ward was more committed to the lie, but after the police started investigating him – watching his home, tapping his phone and even driving away his clients – he threatened to go public. He was kind (or foolish) enough to warn Timothy Bligh, private secretary to Prime Minister Harold Macmillan, of his change in heart, who duly reported it to his boss.

In a letter revealed only recently, Bligh wrote that he'd also consulted with the police and an arrest could be made "in a week or so". Veteran human rights barrister Geoffrey Robertson called this letter "a smoking gun that provides clear evidence of interference by the Prime Minister".

Faced with mounting pressure from the opposition, media and public, Profumo finally confessed to Bligh on 4 June and resigned the next day. The press was livid, with even *The Times*, one of the cornerstones of the establishment, calling it "a great tragedy for the probity of public life".

But the real tragedy is what happened next. While Profumo was able to slink away out of the spotlight with his wife remaining at his side (even receiving an OBE in 1975), others weren't so lucky.

Keeler was eviscerated in the press and was soon after imprisoned for six months after she committed perjury during the trial of another ex-boyfriend, Aloysius "Lucky" Gordon. Two later marriages failed and most of the money she'd made from the affair was spent on legal fees.

During the 1970s, she stated, "I was not living. I was surviving."

Ward suffered an even worse fate. Arrested on trumped up charges days after Profumo resigned, he appeared at the Old Bailey in late July 1963 charged with living off immoral earnings – supposedly of Keeler and other girls, including Mandy Rice-Davies.

Of course, the girls that stayed with him were not prostitutes, and if anything, Ward kept them in the black through his substantial earnings as an osteopath.

But the powers-that-be needed a scapegoat. Judge Archie Marshall refused to let the jury know that Keeler had given false evidence during Gordon's trial and even openly mocked Ward for being abandoned by the same high society that had gladly accepted his party invites.

Not waiting to hear the verdict – which was unsurprisingly guilty – Ward took an overdose of sleeping pills on the night of 30 July and slipped into a coma. Four days later he was dead.

The government he left behind went into full panic mode. As late as mid-March, Macmillan had dismissed the story as mere tabloid tattle, writing in his diary "I was forced to spend a great deal of today over a silly scrape."

Three months later, the "silly scrape" was threatening to bring his administration down.

To appease the nation, the PM had Lord Denning open an inquiry. Denning was Master of the Rolls, making him the second most senior judge in the country and an establishment favourite. Shockingly, his eagerly anticipated report found no evidence of security leaks or other ministerial scandals.

Today, historians tend to agree with the former, but are increasingly sceptical of the latter.

Macmillan stepped down soon after, citing ill health, and was replaced by Sir Alec Douglas-Home, who went on to lose the 1964 election to Harold Wilson.

The Tories' 13-year reign had been ended, thanks in part to one of their own. The press had a new lease of life, suddenly aware they could actually report the things they'd discovered. And Britain's interest in sex may well have been awakened.

Keeler certainly thought so, stating poignantly: "They wanted to hear about the sex, of course. But not the rest. No one wanted to hear the rest."

Q7

Q12

Cameron's government featured in whose book?

Harold Wilson was one of how many Labour PMs?

THE TOUGH *THIS* ENGLAND POLITICS QUIZ

Test your knowledge on the corridors of power

GOSSIP AND SCANDAL

1. Name the Somerton and Frome MP who was pictured, in spring 2022, next to an upturned baking tray with lines of white powder on top, which his father-in-law said he thought was an April Fool's joke?

2. Which government minister was on the front page of *The Sun* wearing a Chelsea strip, and had to resign over his extra-marital affair with actress Antonia de Sancha?

3. The John Major government launched a campaign to clean up politics and get back to family values, but what was it called?

4. Which Liberal party leader was arrested and tried for hiring a hitman to murder his lover, Norman Scott?

5. One of the most unusual items in the MPs expenses scandal was claimed by the late Sir Peter Viggers, who was then asked to

resign by David Cameron. What was this item?

6. Which Labour MP faked his own death and went to Australia, where he was seen behaving strangely and was mistaken for Lord Lucan?

7. *Diary of an MP's Wife* lifted the lid on the David Cameron government and Boris Johnson's rise. Who wrote it?

8. Which former London Mayor is known for his

love of reptiles and amphibia and was even the subject of a feature called "Me and My Newt" in *The Guardian*?

9. Which politician was caught on CCTV kissing his aide during the pandemic, and what is her name?

10. Which Labour big cheese known for his two Jaguars was also known for his affair with his diary secretary Tracey Temple?

DATES, STATS AND HISTORY

11. Who was Britain's first Prime Minister?

12. How many Labour Prime Ministers have there been in total?

13. Who was the last non-Labour, non-Conservative Prime Minister, and when did he serve?

14. How many Prime

Ministers has HM Queen Elizabeth II worked with during her reign?

15. Which Prime Minister was the only 20th-century PM to have held all four offices of state – Chancellor of the Exchequer, Home Secretary, Foreign Secretary and Prime Minister?

16. Who have been our top three longest-serving Prime Ministers?

17. There were two elections in the last century where turnout was above 80 per cent of the population. Which elections were they?

18. Margaret Thatcher became PM in 1979, but in which year did she

become leader of the Conservative party?

19. How many Prime Ministers have been educated at Oxford University?

20. Which Prime Minister has served the most terms in office at four, finishing his last term when he was in his 80s?

The Queen with one of her how many PMs?

True or False: he went to lockdown parties?

Power agreement over an American Hot?

BEHIND THE POWER

21. Which cabinet minister was credited as the architect of Margaret Thatcher's revolution, and also as a key player in her downfall?

22. Which current cabinet minister appeared on *I'm a Celebrity... Get Me Out of Here!* where she was voted off first for failing to secure any food for her camp-mates?

23. Winston Churchill's war cabinet was made up of five politicians. Name three of them.

24. Which Labour cabinet member was known for his eyebrows, lost two leadership contests and became known as one of the best Prime Ministers Britain never had?

25. Edward Smith Stanley's government collapsed in 1852 after his Chancellor's budget was rejected by the house. Who was his Chancellor, who later led the country?

26. In the 1997 general election, which government heavyweight

lost his seat to the unknown Stephen Twigg?

27. Which Foreign Secretary resigned in 1938 in protest at Neville Chamberlain's appeasement of Nazi Germany?

28. Who was Tony Blair's Northern Ireland Secretary who helped broker the 1998 Good Friday Agreement?

29. Who was the Energy and Climate Change Secretary in David Cameron's government before becoming the Home Secretary in Theresa May's government, then Equalities Secretary, then Work and Pensions Secretary before standing down in 2019?

30. Name both the Defence Secretary who resigned in protest over the Westland Helicopters affair and the Trade and Industry Secretary who resigned 15 days later in 1986?

TRUE OR FALSE?

31. Edward Heath was known as The Grocer in *Private Eye* magazine.

32. "You've never had it so good" was the motto of Anthony Eden's government.

33. Winston Churchill's second term of office started in 1951.

34. The Labour Isn't Working poster appeared in 1999.

35. "Hug a Hoodie" was a landmark campaign which was started by Theresa May in a speech in the Bluewater Shopping Centre in 2012.

36. Policemen are known as "bobbies" after Prime Minister Robert Peel, who created the first modern police force.

37. Prime Minister Boris Johnson attended parties during the pandemic lockdown and has been fined by the police.

38. The Blair-Brown deal, known as the "Pizza Express Pact" was struck during a dinner in the Islington branch of Pizza Express.

39. Lloyd George was nicknamed "the Goat" because of his love for the green, green grass of home.

40. The 18-year-old Queen Victoria had a crush on her first Prime Minister Lord Melbourne.

Answers on page 107

TRAIN OF *Dreams*

John Greeves recounts the luxurious and eventful history of the Orient Express

ONE hundred and forty years ago, a revolutionary train service was established which would change the face of rail travel forever. Since its creation in 1883, the Orient Express has been inextricably linked to luxury, intrigue and exotic travel.

The passenger lists read like a who's who, with the Aga Khan, Haile Selassie, Leopold III and the Duke of York (later George VI) all having ridden on the trains. Multimillionaire travellers over the years included Alfred de Rothschild, the famous Parisian banker, American industrialist Andrew Carnegie and President Herbert Hoover. Authors such as F. Scott Fitzgerald and Agatha Christie also became converts to this grand form of travel, and Christie once wrote, "All my life I had wanted to go on the Orient Express. When I had travelled to France or Spain or Italy, the Orient Express had often been standing at Calais and I had longed to climb up into it." Her 1934 novel, *Murder on the Orient Express*, inspired by the various trips she had taken on the service, brought that desire to millions of readers.

Other frequent passengers included musicians such as Gustav Mahler and world-renowned performers and celebrities including Sarah Bernhardt, Isadora Duncan, Marlene Dietrich and Maurice Chevalier. King Leopold had a private carriage just for the use of his mistress, while Edward VIII often travelled in his bachelor days on the services to Vienna

nightspots such as Chat Noir and the Cocotte under the pretext that he was consulting a famous Viennese physician.

I was fortunate enough to take a trip on the modern day Orient Express service, the Venice Simplon Orient Express, shortly after it first began, stepping aboard a resplendent 1920s cream and brown Pullman carriage named Minerva from London Victoria to Paris. From boyhood I had longed to make this trip after seeing *From Russia with Love*, with James Bond alongside Tatiana Romanova travelling on the Orient Express from Istanbul to Trieste, with a spectre assassin hot on their heels.

On the day of my departure, some of my fellow passengers were dressed in period costumes of the '20s and '30s. As I boarded, I looked forward to unhurried travel in a sumptuous cabin, evoking a sense of nostalgia for a time when luxury, comfort and service reigned supreme. Each carriage was restored to its heyday with delicate polished Art Deco wood panelling of rosewood and ash. On the first leg of the journey I enjoyed tea and a luxurious champagne brunch as the train ambled through the English countryside while I sat back in a comfortable armchair.

Today passengers travel through the Eurotunnel, but in the early days of the VSOE, they travelled to Folkstone and boarded a VIP lounge on a cross-Channel ship, and luggage, boarding cards and passports were all attended to by a train official while you relaxed.

When I reached France on my

journey, the continental train, made up of former sleeping cars and dining cars of the Compagnie Internationale des Wagon-Lits, awaited. Dinner back then was a memorable affair in the beautiful Art Deco dining car, and I was now greeted by the same gleaming crystal, white damask table clothes and Limoges China, while Michelin standard Nouvelle cuisine was served, accompanied by the finest selection of wines.

Sartorial elegance reigned supreme, with women bedecked in glittering evening gowns and men in tuxedos or even Nehru suits.

The social hub of the train has always been the bar. It was here I learned a little more about my fellow passengers, while ordering a signature cocktail (shaken not stirred) with the pianist playing in the background. Everyone I met had a special reason for being on

the train, like the young couple who had just got married, some celebrating a special anniversary, a retirement, or a big birthday. Whatever the reason, we all seemed to share the same dream, knowing this was the closest we would ever get to the golden age of travel. We had all experienced the pinnacle of luxury reminiscent of a bygone age, but better still had forged lasting memories from this trip of a lifetime.

The original Orient Express train service was the brainchild of Georges Nagelmackers, who established the French rail operator Compagnie Internationale des Wagons-Lits and ensured that the Orient Express would become the "queen of the rails". The extravagant service carried passengers across Europe, most famously travelling in the 1920s from the Gare de l'Est in Paris to

the Sirkeci Terminal in Istanbul through the recently completed Simplon Tunnel. This saw the beginning of the Simplon Orient Express service, which was followed by the Arlberg Orient Express service, running through Switzerland, in the 1930s. All the Orient Express services provided an international cachet of opulence and inspired the setting for novels, films and television features alike.

The original Orient Express train consisted of a locomotive, a mail wagon, sleeping cars, a restaurant, and a four wheel fourgon for passenger baggage, food, crates of wines, champagne, port, brandy and liqueurs. Life on board was comparable to any top luxury hotel. A drawing room existed for the ladies, furnished in exquisite taste, with Louis XV chairs and taborets, chaise longues and silk drapes covering the windows. The

gentlemen's smoking room was similarly enriched with leather armchairs, footstools, bookcases filled to the brim with reading matter and international newspapers that created the ambience of a London club.

The dining saloons lit by huge chandeliers had panelling of the finest mahogany and teak inlaid with rosewood marquetry, with etchings from artists Delacroix and Decamps on the walls. Tables were laid with spotless white damask cloths, silver cutlery and napkins folded into butterflies, while wine was served in the finest Baccarat crystal from the Lunéville factory.

Dinner consisted of ten courses and lasted up to three hours. The quality of food was so good that King Edward VII later asked the Orient Express's chef to become his own personal royal cook. He   >

A grand suite on board the Venice Simplon Orient Express

An external view of the VSOE

The train's state of the art bathrooms

A luxury dinner carriage

Experience only the best service on board

declined, saying his wife didn't want to leave France. However, generally the train management prided themselves on acceding to any passenger request, whether it came from a maharajah, a courtesan or a king. When temperamental Australian soprano Dame Nellie Melba demanded she be served the same Pêche Melba the chef at London's Savoy Hotel had created for her, the Orient Express chef discovered he was out of peaches and used pears for the dessert instead. And so the Poires Melba was born, much to Nellie Melba's delight.

However, despite its opulence, life on board the Orient Express wasn't without incident. In 1891 the front of the train was partially derailed in Thrace mid-journey

and a major train robbery ensued with the equivalent of almost £1m stolen from passengers, with further sums later paid to ransom individuals. On another occasion, King Ferdinand of Bulgaria insisted on driving the train through his country himself, which he proceeded to do at perilous speeds.

Another incident saw Paul Deschanel, then President of France, fall head-first from the train while trying to unfasten a window, mistakenly opening the door instead. He picked himself up, bruised and battered, but later faced a much harder task trying to convince a rail official that he was indeed the President of France. Apparently, as he stood shivering in his dirty pyjamas with one

slipper missing in front of the official, he was greeted with a sneering reply, "Oh, really, then I must be Emperor Napoleon . . ."

Despite Agatha Christie's invention, one thing which did not in fact occur on the Orient Express was murder. However, arms dealer Basil Zaharoff, one of the richest men in the world during his lifetime and described as "the merchant of death", did save the Duchess of Villafranca from murder on board. On a honeymoon gone wrong, the Duchess's new husband, the Duke of Marchena, attempted to stab her to death. Luckily Zaharoff intervened, and the couple later married while the Duke of Marchena lived out the rest of his life in a psychiatric hospital.

The onboard bar, the train's social hub

A bed fit for a king in a grand suite

Intricate details throughout the train

Suites are complete with decanter stands

The train attracted all sorts of drama and over the years it earned the name "Spies' Express", having become a magnet for espionage. Famous spies such as Mata Hari and Lord Robert Baden-Powell travelled on the trains, using them as a base for their work. Baden-Powell famously posed as a lepidopterist in the Balkans in order to make intricate coded sketches of the fortifications he spotted along the Dalmatian Coast while on board, which he disguised as butterfly sketches.

Today the only Orient Express train service remaining is the Venice Simplon Orient Express, with all other services having sadly ceased operation. Luxury hospitality and leisure company Belmond has owned and operated the VSOE since its inaugural journey in 1982 from London to Venice via Milan.

In the UK, Pullman carriages are used for the service but in continental Europe sleeping and dining cars of the former Compagnie Internationale des Wagons-Lits are utilised, which all date from the 1920s and 30s. The VSOE offers spectacular journeys across Europe, many leaving from London Victoria, including a once a year special journey from Paris to Istanbul following the famous cross-continental route of the original Simplon Orient Express service of the 1920s. The continental leg consists of 18 carriages, including 12 original sleeper carriages, three dining cars, a bar with a mini grand piano, two carriages for staff, plus a storage room for supplies.

Cabins are now available in three different sizes: twin cabins, cabin suites and a grand suite. A twin cabin is converted from a cosy lounge during the day to a bedroom at night. A cabin suite is twice the size and the final six grand suites are much larger and more ornate, each named after a European city. The epitome of luxury, the grand suites offer hand-embroidered cushions, intricately carved marquetry suites with double or twin bed layouts, a drawing room saloon with a sofa, an en suite bathroom and underfloor heating.

For more information about the Orient Express train services running today, visit belmond.com.

Images: Belmond, Shutterstock

Winter

By Andrea Hazeldine

Red berries deck the holly,
Frost on the trees.
Crisp and crunchy,
A path of fallen leaves.

A soft white embrace,
As charming as it seems,
Creates the lovely picture,
The perfect winter scene.

Sheep on the hills near Clun in Shropshire

AUTUMN TO WINTER

Events of the season, Frankie Howerd remembered, the foliage of winter and the birth of the supermarket

>

AUTUMN TO WINTER

Katherine Sorrell on tar barrel racing, Santa dashes, one of the world's oldest car rallies and Black History Month

OCTOBER 2023

Nick Ferrari and Boris Johnson

HAPPY 50TH BIRTHDAY TO LBC

It was the birth of commercial radio in the UK. London Broadcasting Company, Britain's first legal commercial independent radio station (there were plenty of "pirate" radio stations before then) began broadcasting in October 1973. It all started at 6am with the *Morning Show*, presented by David Jessel.

NOTTINGHAM GOOSE FAIR

This travelling fair, which has a history going back more than 700 years and attracts a crowd of around 450,000, usually arrives in Nottingham for five days every October. It features more than 80 large rides, around 40 children's rides, as well as side shows and food stalls. It's one of the largest funfairs in the UK and gets its name from the days when traders would march their geese to Nottingham market to sell. **facebook.com/NottinghamGooseFair**

GREAT NORTHERN CONTEMPORARY CRAFT FAIR

Whether jewellery or ceramics, furniture or prints, the North's foremost contemporary craft fair offers the chance to buy direct from designer-makers, all selected for their excellence, at the Victoria Baths in Hathersage, Manchester. **greatnorthernevents.co.uk**

WINTER DROVING

Turn back your clock four centuries: this Cumbrian cultural event harks back to the tradition of herding animals over long distances to market. A celebration of all things rural, the Penrith festival includes a busy food and drink market, various street performers, live music and a torch-lit procession. **edenarts.co.uk/projects/winter-droving**

HORSE OF THE YEAR SHOW

In the biggest week of the year for equestrian entertainment, the Horse of the Year Show fills 50 acres of Birmingham's NEC with thrilling competitions and breathtaking displays of horsemanship for five days every October. It includes finals to many national showjumping championships. **hoys.co.uk**

Over the jumps at the NEC

TRAFALGAR DAY

The most important day in the Naval calendar, and one that defined British sailing for hundreds of years, Trafalgar Day commemorates Nelson's victory at the Battle of Trafalgar in October 1805. A ceremony takes place in Portsmouth on board *HMS Victory*, while in London, on the closest Sunday to 21 Oct, hundreds of Sea Cadets march down The Mall to Buckingham Palace – a stirring sight. **sea-cadets.org**

Sea cadets in London

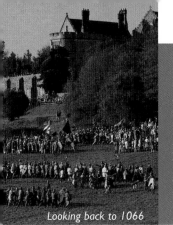
Looking back to 1066

BATTLE OF HASTINGS RE-ENACTMENT

English Heritage's biggest and most popular event of the year attracts an audience of thousands to watch armies clash on the very spot in Battle, East Sussex, where King Harold and Duke William fought on that fateful day in 1066. There's plenty more on offer in this lively weekend, too: discover what life was like in an 11th-century army, see the weapons, armour and clothing worn by Saxon and Norman soldiers and meet falconers and their majestic birds of prey. **english-heritage.org.uk**

CHELTENHAM LITERATURE FESTIVAL

One of the oldest literary events in the world, the Literature Festival at Cheltenham celebrates the joy of the written and spoken word with the best new voices in fiction and poetry alongside literary greats. During the 10-day programme, there are debates, interviews and workshops, while the Literature for Schools programme inspires more than 9,000 school children with a love of books. **cheltenhamfestivals. com/literature**

APPLE TASTING DAY

Apple Day celebrations take place throughout the country in October, raising awareness not only of the importance of orchards to our landscape and culture, but also of the provenance and traceability of food. At Blackmoor Estate, Hampshire, you can taste a wide variety of its old and new apples and pears. Experts are at hand to identify mystery apples, trees and plants are on sale, and there's also a rural craft fair and demonstrations. **blackmoorestate.co.uk**

Varieties to check out

WORLD CONKER CHAMPIONSHIPS

Held in Southwick, Northamptonshire, on the second Sunday of October each year, the competition has taken place since 1965. These days thousands come to watch in the grounds of the Shuckburgh Arms, and entrants jet in from around the world. There's entertainment, too, and plenty of money raised for the visually impaired. **worldconkerchampionships.com**

Ready for battle

THE GREAT FRAMLINGHAM SAUSAGE FESTIVAL

Hurray for the British banger! This one-day festival celebrates the sausages made in East Anglia using local ingredients and recipes. There are food stands, live music, workshops and children's events. **framlinghamsausagefestival.com**

BLACK HISTORY MONTH

The first Black History Week was in the USA in 1926, established by Dr Carter G. Woodson, the son of former slaves who became only the second African American to be awarded a doctorate from Harvard University. He worked tirelessly to promote black history in American schools, though it was not until 1970 that the event was expanded to a month, held since 1976 in February. The first Black History Month was held in the UK in October 1987. It is intended to share, celebrate and understand the impact of black history and culture, to recognise the contribution and achievements of people with African or Caribbean heritage, and to offer an opportunity to learn more about the effects of racism in our society. Today, it has become an important date in the cultural calendar of many of the UK's museums, galleries and local authorities, and schools take the opportunity to focus on studying black British history. See listings for an event near you. *blackhistorymonth.org.uk/listings*

TENTERDEN FOLK FESTIVAL

This friendly festival takes place over four days, including the first Saturday of October, celebrating folk song, music, dance, crafts and traditions. As well as the main concerts and special shows, there are barn dances, sing-a-rounds, music sessions and workshops. **tenterdenfolkfestival. com/TFF**

BIRMINGHAM COMEDY FESTIVAL

A 10-day, city-wide extravaganza, one of the longest-running comedy festivals in the UK attracts big names. Stand-up is at its core, but you can also enjoy cabaret, improv, music, pub quizzes, puppet shows, film screenings, poetry readings and more. **bhamcomfest. co.uk**

CHANGE TAKES TRUE CHARACTER
PROUD TO SUPPORT BLACK HISTORY TODAY AND EVERY DAY

Coutts bank marks Black History Month

DOCTOR WHO TURNS 60

On 23 November 1963 the BBC broadcast the first ever episode of *Doctor Who*, starring William Hartnell. The much-loved adventure set across time and space is now the world's longest-running science-fiction drama.

Meeting the Daleks in Cardiff

LEWES BONFIRE CELEBRATIONS

Bonfire celebrations are held around Sussex from early September until the end of November, marking both Guy Fawkes Night and the burning of local Protestant martyrs. The many Sussex bonfire societies stage atmospheric torch-lit processions through these historic towns and villages, featuring burning barrels, costumed marchers, drums and giant (sometimes controversial) celebrity effigies. Enormous bonfires are the focal point and everything ends with a huge fireworks display. There are always huge crowds. **lewesbonfirecelebrations.com**

WINTER LIGHT FESTIVALS

Ready, get set, glow. A huge number of dazzling light displays, trails and installations illuminate city-centre architecture and historic venues up and down the country each winter. Thousands of bulbs, lasers, sculptures, twinkles and sparkles make up tunnels, glowing flowers, cute animals, soaring snowflakes and all kinds of imaginative escapism. In London alone there's Kew Gardens, Wembley Park, Kenwood House, Canary Wharf and Eltham Palace, to name a few, as well as the usual stunning displays in Oxford Street and around. Elsewhere there are spectacular winter light festivals at Blenheim Palace, Waddesdon Manor, Dunham Massey, Castle Howard, the botanic gardens at Wakehurst, the National Arboretum at Westonbirt, Longleat and RHS Gardens. Book early to avoid disappointment.

Magic at Kew

TURNING THE DEVIL'S STONE

It measures about 6ft by 4ft and weighs around a ton – and no one knows how the huge lump of rock known as the Devil's Stone found its way to the village square in Shebbear, Devon. What the villagers do know is that if they don't "turn" the stone each year, on 5 November, bad luck will ensue. The ceremony begins at around 8pm. **shebbearvillage.co.uk**

TAR BARRELS

The West Country has a long history of torchlight processions and burning barrels, but in Devon's Ottery St Mary there's a twist – the full-sized, tar-lined, lit barrels are carried on the participants'

Hot work in Ottery St Mary

shoulders on 5 November each year. Generations of local families take part, and as the day and evening progresses, the barrels get larger and heavier. Not one for the faint-hearted, that's for sure. Spectators are advised to wear warm, old clothing, and no young children or dogs are allowed nearby. **tarbarrels.co.uk**

WINCHESTER CATHEDRAL CHRISTMAS MARKET

Inspired by traditional German Christmas markets, and widely considered one of Europe's best, this market attracts more than 400,000 visitors. Hand-picked exhibitors offer exclusive gifts and seasonal treats, based in wooden chalets in the cathedral's Inner Close. **christmas.winchester-cathedral.org.uk**

ANTROBUS SOUL CAKERS

The ancient tradition of "souling" (a precursor to trick or treating, marking the dates around All Souls' Day on 2 November) has largely died out, but a troupe of enthusiasts from Antrobus, Cheshire, is keeping it alive. The Antrobus Soul Cakers perform a mumming play in local pubs over six nights in early November, raising money for charity. There is much hilarity . . . **facebook.com/soulcakers**

SKINNINGROVE BONFIRE

A fireworks display followed by an enormous bonfire – not so different from many 5 November celebrations, you may think. But in the village of Skinningrove, North Yorkshire, each year the bonfire in question is built carefully on the beach to a specific, locally themed design. Started in 1982 as a simple village arts project, it has grown into a spectacle that attracts crowds of several thousand. **skinningrovebonfire.org.uk**

THE LORD MAYOR'S SHOW

A fixture of London life for more than 800 years, the Lord Mayor's Show has its origins in King John's issue of a Royal Charter that allowed the City of London to elect its own Mayor each year. A condition was that the Mayor should travel upriver to Westminster and swear loyalty to the crown. The Mayor's journey was the celebrity spectacle of its day, and over the years it has featured in the plays of Shakespeare, the diaries of Pepys and the adventures of James Bond, as well as, of course, the pantomime story of Dick Whittington (who really was the Mayor of London three times). **lordmayorsshow.london**

The Lord Mayor's Show

ST NICHOLAS FAIR

One of the longest-running in the country, York's Christmas market takes place for six weeks across the festive period, featuring alpine chalets with twinkling lights, a vintage carousel and plenty of mulled wine. **visityork.org/christmas**

LONDON TO BRIGHTON VETERAN CAR RUN

It's billed as the world's longest-running and greatest motoring celebration, in which hundreds of splendid automobiles, all built before 1905, set out from London's Hyde Park at sunrise on the first Sunday in November and (hopefully) chug all the way along the 60-mile route to a grand finish on the seafront in Brighton. Eccentric and charming, the run attracts vehicles from around the world, and huge crowds along the route. **veterancarrun.com**

Going vintage on the streets of Streatham

Carnival time in Bridgwater

BRIDGWATER GUY FAWKES CARNIVAL

Somerset, too, has a carnival tradition dating back to the 1600s, when many parts of the county commemorated the Gunpowder Plot. Today, they combine open-air entertainment, fairs, street food and parades of illuminated carts. Up to 100 feet long, the carts are covered in intricate, themed designs featuring moving parts and thousands of light bulbs – all designed and built by members of the local carnival clubs. The carnivals visit Somerset towns on a circuit each autumn, with Bridgwater taking place on the first Saturday in November. The procession takes about two hours. Stay on till the grand finale when a line-up of people simultaneously set off large fireworks, held above their heads, creating a trail of fire. **bridgwatercarnival.org.uk**

The National Service of Remembrance

ARMISTICE DAY

At 11am on the 11th day of the 11th month, the nation holds a two-minute silence to remember those who gave their lives in war. "Armistice" is Latin for "to stand (still) arms", and this day commemorates the agreement, begun at 11am on 11 November 1918, to end the fighting in the First World War. The National Service of Remembrance at the Cenotaph in London, attended by senior members of the Royal Family and the government and involving a march-past of up to 10,000 war veterans, is held on Remembrance Sunday, the closest Sunday to 11 November. **britishlegion.org.uk**

>

THE 70TH ANNIVERSARY OF WINSTON CHURCHILL'S NOBEL PRIZE

Winston's prestigious prize

In recognition of his mastery of historical and biographical description, as well as "brilliant oratory in defending exalted human values", Sir Winston Churchill was awarded the Nobel Prize in Literature on 10 December 1953. His wife Clementine accepted the prize on his behalf from the King of Sweden in Stockholm, as the former Prime Minister was attending a summit with Dwight Eisenhower in Bermuda. During his lifetime, Churchill wrote 43 book-length works, including one novel, *Savrola*.

80 YEARS AGO – ANIMALS HONOURED FOR WARTIME EFFORTS

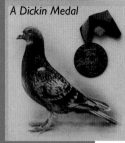
A Dickin Medal

On 2 December 1943, the pigeons White Vision, Winkie and Tyke became the first recipients of the PDSA Dickin Medal, the animals' Victoria Cross, instituted to acknowledge outstanding acts of bravery or dedication to duty by animals in war. The birds each contributed to the rescue of stranded RAF aircrew by delivering messages under "exceptionally difficult circumstances".

BOXING DAY SQUIRT

Members of the volunteer fire brigade in Geddington, Northamptonshire, have their annual Boxing Day "Squirt" – essentially a water fight against a friendly local fire station rival, in which a beer barrel is suspended from a cable over the local river and the two teams attempt to push the barrel over the heads of their opposition using their hose jets. Visitors are advised to wear waterproof clothing . . .
gvfb.org/squirt

MONTOL FESTIVAL

This six-day arts and community festival held in Penzance, Cornwall, celebrates the winter solstice and the county's midwinter customs. After lantern and mask-making workshops, carol services, storytelling, plays and late-night shopping, the festival culminates in Montol Eve on 21 December. The main draw is a lantern-lit parade through the town, with participants dressed in mock formal wear and masks, taking part in "Guise" dancing.
montolfestival.co.uk

WINTER WATCH AND SATURNALIA PARADE

Out and about on the streets of Chester, this midwinter spectacle features a re-enactment of the Winter Watch, a ceremony dating from the 15th century when the good burghers would put the keys to the city in the safe hands of the City Watch. The party starts when the Lord of Misrule and a mischievous gathering of fire breathers, devils, skeletons, ice queens, Jack Frosts and even bloodthirsty cooks (bearing a head on a platter), dance around the city centre. There is an amazing finale of firebreathing.
midsummerwatch.co.uk/ winter-watch-parade

THE GREAT CHRISTMAS PUDDING RACE

Taking place in London's Covent Garden, teams in fancy dress race (on behalf of Cancer Research UK) to complete a festive obstacle course while balancing a Christmas pudding on a tray.
xmaspuddingrace.org.uk

Balancing a pudding in London

TREE DRESSING

Taking place during National Tree Week on the first weekend in December, tree dressing is based on many ancient customs from all over the world. Communities across the UK gather and celebrate by "dressing" a tree in ribbons, bunting or other decorations.
commonground.org.uk/ tree-dressing-day

MATLOCK BATH RAFT EVENT

Raising money for the RNLI, this Boxing Day "race" for decorated rafts attracts fearless, water-loving and slightly bonkers entrants from all over the country, who float the River Derwent from Cawdor Quarry in Matlock, Derbyshire, to Cromford Meadows, watched by a huge turnout of spectators. **matlockraftevent.co.uk**

WHITE CHRISTMAS DIP

Bracing sea swims take place the length and breadth of the country on Christmas Day, Boxing Day and New Year's Day, with charity fund-raising the name of the game. You can run, walk or scream your way into the water from a beach, harbour, quayside, pier, weir or estuary, while a few festive dips even take place in lidos. The White Christmas Dip, which takes place on Christmas morning on Boscombe Beach near Bournemouth in Dorset, is said to be the UK's biggest charity dip and it's in aid of Macmillan Caring Locally. It's time to freeze your baubles off . . . **whitechristmasdip.co.uk**

Brr, it's cold!

TOM BAWCOCK'S EVE

On the day before Christmas Eve, villagers in Cornwall's picturesque Mousehole celebrate the heroic efforts of legendary Tom Bawcock, who is said to have alleviated a famine by going out to fish in a severe storm. Watch the lantern procession, enjoy the village's famous display of lights, then head to the Ship Inn and you'll be served a slice of "stargazy" pie. **facebook.com/shipinnmousehole**

BURNING THE CLOCKS

A Brighton tradition for two decades, Burning the Clocks takes place every year on 21 December, an antidote to commercial excesses and a way to celebrate the festive season regardless of faith. Attracting thousands of spectators, the event begins with a procession of hand-made paper and willow lanterns, and finishes with a spectacular beach bonfire, plus fireworks accompanied by live music. **facebook.com/burningtheclocks**

A lantern procession

SANTA DASH

The streets of Liverpool

If you can run, walk or drive a sleigh for 5k, then why not join in with a fancy-dress "Santa Dash" this December? They take place all over England, in aid of good causes and festive cheer. Liverpool's Santa Dash is the country's biggest and longest-established, attracting thousands of runners to jog a course through the city and raise money for the Alder Hey Children's Charity. **btrliverpool.com/santa-dash-event**

TAR BAR'L

It's possible this spectacular New Year's Eve fire festival in the town of Allendale, Northumberland, began as far back as the Middle Ages; it has certainly been celebrated for at least 160 years as a way of seeing out the old year and welcoming in the new. The focal point of the night of music and dancing is a procession of 45 "guisers": local men who wear colourful fancy dress and carry whisky barrels filled with burning tar. **visitnorthumberland.com/explore/seasons/winter/tar-barl**

NEW YEAR'S EVE FIREWORKS

The UK's largest annual fireworks display takes place on New Year's Eve in London, with colourful pyrotechnics over the London Eye dazzling spectators to the accompaniment of Big Ben's "bongs". At the far end of the country, thousands gather in St Ives in Cornwall, where the streets are thronged with revellers and a fireworks display takes place on the harbour. It's said to be the second biggest fancy dress party in England. Bideford and Dartmouth in Devon also have huge outdoor fancy-dress parties that rival St Ives, with fireworks at midnight.

Major cities such as Manchester, Gateshead, Birmingham, Nottingham and Liverpool each have huge, organised displays to mark the start of the New Year, while Flamborough, Yorkshire, celebrates its Viking heritage with a New Year's Eve fire festival.

Fireworks above Big Ben

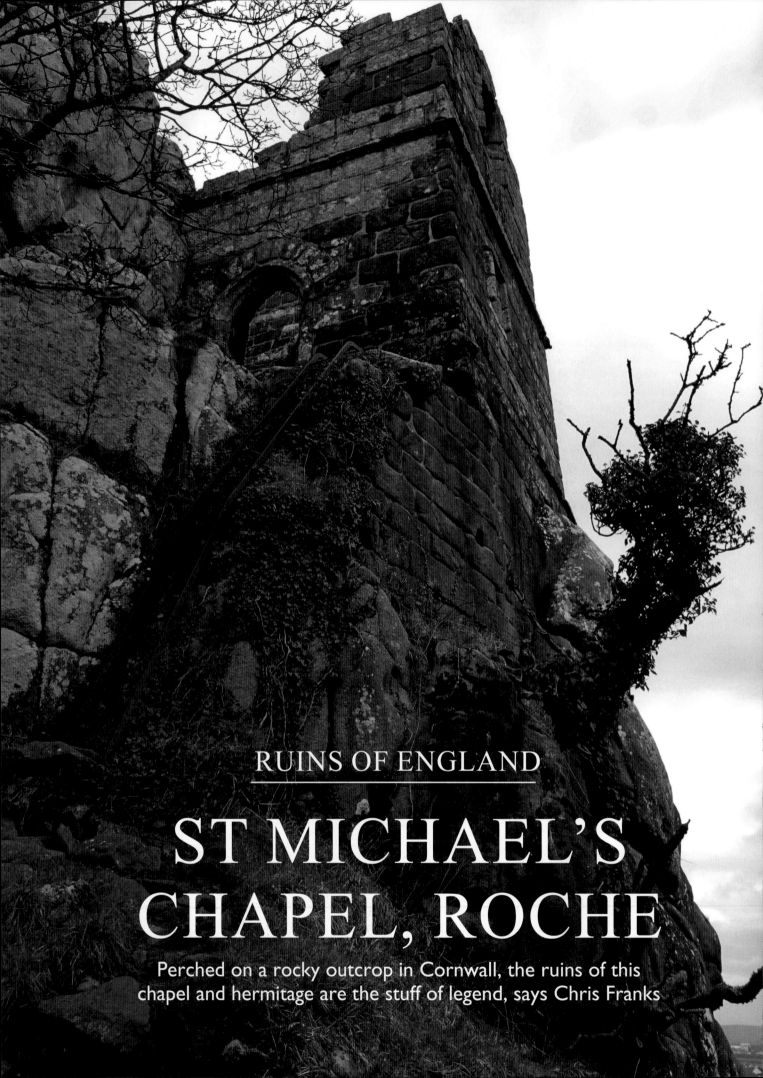

RUINS OF ENGLAND

ST MICHAEL'S CHAPEL, ROCHE

Perched on a rocky outcrop in Cornwall, the ruins of this
chapel and hermitage are the stuff of legend, says Chris Franks

The ruin overlooks Bodmin Moor

YOU approach warily. The crows are watching, their caws and screeches like warnings as they loiter among the crags. All around is the vast emptiness of Bodmin Moor, and in the short climb up from the road the wind has gathered.

It is very easy to see the fascination for the place – how it would draw people. You have to crane your neck almost vertically just to look at it. Balanced impossibly on the summit of a 66-foot rock pillar, and guarded by cliffs on all sides, this is the ruin of St Michael's Chapel.

St Michael's lies near the village of Roche in Cornwall. The pillar of tourmaline quartz on which it stands has been a social and ceremonial focal point since Neolithic times. The chapel was built in 1409 and had two rooms on separate floors, the upper being the chapel itself, and the lower serving as accommodation.

While the western end has almost completely disappeared, the east wall, the one visible from below, still stands to its original height. When the chapel fell into ruin is unknown, but it has been abandoned for centuries.

On one side of the ruin the cliffs yield a little, and a steep winding track leads to a 25-foot iron ladder. As you start to climb, it clangs like a submerged bell. The crows scream their disapproval and take flight. At the top is the entrance and, inside, a second ladder takes you up to the chapel level. With the help of a grab bar, you scramble out through a narrow doorway on to the summit.

It is extraordinary – the stuff of myths – and there are many about this place. When fleeing the angry King Mark, tragic lovers Tristan and Isolde are said to have taken refuge here, as did Cornish folklore hero Jan Tregeagle, while being chased by demons. The most enduring legend is of a local man who retired here as a hermit after contracting leprosy. His daughter, Saint Gundred, is said to have brought him water each day from a nearby well, and the popular name of Roche Rock Hermitage comes from this.

Stand and feel the wind crumple around you; listen to it scrape over the broken walls. Gaze through the lifeless chapel window at the sun rising above the distant hills. It's one of those fantastic places that fires the imagination and makes you think for a moment that you want to be there forever.

But the exposure here is stifling. The tiny rock platform hangs in mid-air, with sheer drops all around, waiting for one careless step. Just being here constricts you with anxiety, and for all the beauty, you cannot stay. Some places are just too wild and too remote for people.

Back at the road, the wind eases and your spirit calms as normality returns. The crows gather once more. This is their world now.

Images: Chris Franks

DON'T LAUGH! IT'S FRANKIE HOWERD

Amanda Hodges
pays tribute to a
comedy great

WAS there ever such an unlikely or unforgettable comedian as Frankie Howerd? A man consumed by anxiety yet who felt compelled to perform, a true survivor who weathered infinite setbacks galore and a genuine comedy pioneer whose influence remains powerfully palpable today. Every carefully rehearsed appearance would feature the distinctive "oohs", "aahs" and "thrice nays" that would colourfully illustrate a routine of deliciously discursive stories, turned to comedic gold by virtue of his performance skills.

The brashness of his *Up Pompeii* days perhaps obscured his talent. But Howerd was no one-dimensional comedian but a master of stand-up, someone who, as his biographer Graham McCann rightly asserts, "stamped his signature upon each of the media he mastered".

"Nervy – that was me. Nerves were the only things that came easily!" Howerd recalled in his candid and self-deprecating autobiography, *On The Way I Lost It*. Born in York in 1917 but brought up in Eltham, Francis Alick Howard (changed to "e" later) was, according to his autobiography, "incredibly shy and withdrawn. Paradoxically, despite a dread of heights . . . I'd climb trees – just to be alone in my private, dream world."

Taken by his mother to see pantomime at Woolwich (his father was a soldier in the Royal Artillery) Howerd was captivated. The other, more unusual passion of his early life was religion.

"I decided to become a saint. Why? Because Heaven seemed to offer an even happier world than

With famous cook Fanny Cradock

the theatre . . . I really thought in those pre-teen years that if I lived a good, pure life I could end up as St Francis of Eltham and go to Heaven!"

Strangely enough, his religious fervour led directly to acting as he joined the church drama society and began appearing in plays. After one such endeavour someone backstage said casually, "You should be an actor" and, as he'd later recall, "these words acted as an instant catalyst . . . It was an unlikely proposition, an excruciatingly shy, stammering and introspective youth joining what in many ways is the most extrovert of professions!"

He began acting at school, took lessons from London County Council and tried out for RADA. His failure to clinch this after an audition prompted what would become a familiar career pattern for the resourceful Howerd. Bereft, he'd wept, then re-thought his plans.

"Comedy, is that the alternative?" he pondered. "If you're not meant to be a great Shakespearean are you meant to be a comedian?"

He left grammar school, took menial jobs to subsist, then, as war dawned, failed an audition for

ENSA (the actors entertainment unit) and was drafted for military service. It was during his army years that his distinctive comedic style began to take shape. Introduced as "Frankie" during wartime performances (he never missed a stage opportunity), the name he considered babyish stuck.

Howerd realised that he could not simply replicate material popular at the time. "In those days comics were very precise . . . they were word perfect" and entertained an audience from afar with polish and slickly rehearsed scripts. His intense nerves precluded this. "My nervous, stammering delivery was a bit different," so he devised a way to turn his weaknesses into his strengths. "I told stories of misadventure in the form of a cosy gossip, as though leaning over an invisible garden fence or chatting to cronies in the local pub."

It became beautifully honed over the course of his career. Writer and comedian Barry Cryer would talk of Howerd's later skill with awe, what he termed the camouflage of "apparent waffle – he was like a tightrope walker, you thought he's going to fall off in a minute, and then, suddenly – bang. He knew >

FRANKIE'S CAREER

1917: Born in York. Soon moves to Eltham, London, as father is stationed with Royal Artillery.

1940: Begins military service during World War II. Stationed on a boat off Normandy during D-Day, starts regular performing in the army and acquires the stage name "Frankie".

1946: Gets his first big professional break, working on radio programme *Variety Bandbox*; this launches his career in spectacular fashion.

1952 & 1955: First television shows, entitled *The Howerd Crowd*, written by longtime collaborator Eric Sykes.

Frankie in Further Up Pompeii

genius for the near-fantastic". The comic portrayed delivering a pair of elephants in the Rockies and even bravely lion-taming, "all surreal, superbly written and perfect for my technique at the time." He was riding the crest of a wave, radio fame bringing numerous opportunities elsewhere; 1948 and 1949 were years of great success, performing at Buckingham Palace and *The Royal Variety Show* alongside childhood idols Max Miller and Jack Benny.

"Compulsive worrier" Howerd was never complacent and in 1951 he quit *Variety Bandbox*, feeling the spectre of staleness encroaching. He was fortunate in having Sykes's loyal services for many ventures including television debut *The Howerd Crowd* and later young scriptwriters Johnny Speight and Hancock creators Galton and Simpson would also pen successful material for him. He dipped his toe into films (appearing first in 1954's *The Runaway Bus* and in the late Sixties would appear in *Carry On Doctor*, but by the end of the 1950s the gloss had worn off and he was seen as yesterday's man, new and sharp young satirists eclipsing him.

Being Howerd, there was always going to be a second act. A memorable appearance presenting at the *Evening Standard* Drama Awards brought forth an invitation from man of the moment Peter Cook to headline his exciting new Establishment Club in London, an opportunity Howerd almost missed, so deeply mired in gloom was he, briefly considering disavowing showbusiness and buying a pub.

Courtesy of material written by Johnny Speight and useful satirical barbs added to the potent Howerd cocktail, he was, to his own great surprise, an instant hit. "It was very odd," Speight recalled, "because

> exactly what he was doing. What he could do with a script was amazing, like all great performers."

Demobbed, Howerd doggedly pursued his dreams, without much success. He threw caution to the wind after a churlish producer for the Jack Payne organisation made him wait for over four hours to be auditioned. Furious, Howerd told him, "I am now going to make you laugh, you clot . . . Because I'm funny, you oaf!"

Amazingly, his approach worked and he gained his first professional engagement in a major revue. Tweaking his surname because he felt there were too many Howards in the profession he began evolving his act, which was far more digressive than anything seen before. "Yet it worked because the ordinary chap I was portraying was imprecise . . . People in real life don't talk as if from scripts and neither did I onstage."

This apparent artlessness was illusion. As Graham McCann recognises, "we were shown only the messiness – merely the 'ums' and 'ers' – while the elaborate pattern – what Howerd liked (in private) to call a beauty of delivery, a beauty of rhythm and timing –

like a piece of music – was kept well-hidden . . ."

In an era of neat patter and professionalism Howerd's casual delivery, appearance and approach was radically different.

After a matter of weeks the astonished Howerd, reeling from actual success, was invited to audition for radio sensation *Variety Bandbox*, one of the most popular programmes of its day. Initial triumph in late 1946 was heady but soon he was getting notes of dwindling popularity so once again the thoughtful Howerd reappraised his act and changed from "visual to vocal clowning" to introduce the intimacy necessary for radio.

In addition to adopting catchphrases like "titter ye not", he found emphasising words helped too. "One of the gimmicks I evolved was to mispronounce certain words in a special way. Thus ladies and gentlemen became ladies and gentle-men, amazed became a-mazed."

Without fresh material he floundered until a fledgling writer called Eric Sykes started writing his scripts; they marked Sykes's professional debut. Howerd acclaimed Sykes's "great inventive

FRANKIE'S CAREER

1954: His film debut in thriller *The Runaway Bus* written to showcase his comedy talents.

1962: Down on his luck, Howerd appears on 26 September at Peter Cook's Establishment Club in London. He is an instant success, leading to a spot on David Frost's satirical show *That Was The Week That Was*.

1963: Lead in the UK production of *A Funny Thing Happened on the Way to the Forum*, Sondheim's comedy musical. He stays with the show until July 1965.

1964-1966: *The Frankie Howerd Show,* written by *Hancock's Half Hour* team runs for 12 episodes

Frankie Howerd running the full gamut of facial expressions during an appearance on television

Britain had just latched on to satire and producers were screaming for 'the new comedy', as they called it. All the agents and producers regarded Frankie as 'old school' but none of the new generation of comedians or writers saw him that way. In fact, we saw him as the perfect vehicle. He could read anything and make it funny."

Such visibility led to Ned Sherrin booking him for popular satire show, *That Was The Week That Was* on 6 April 1963. Courtesy of sharp material, he found his TV career reborn, something consolidated by Galton and Simpson's series *Frankie Howerd*. Off the back of this came the invitation to star on stage, in a UK version of Sondheim's comedy musical set in ancient Rome, *A Funny Thing Happened on the Way to the Forum*. His casting as slave Pseudolos courtesy of a tip from John Gielgud who'd suggested, "The show was pure Frankie without Frankie knowing about it!"

Ahead lay a plethora of opportunities, from a (cut) role in the Beatles film *Help!*, his two *Carry On* appearances and his

small-screen time as lascivious Lurcio in *Up Pompeii*, where he broke the fourth wall by making asides to the studio audience; something innately suited to his confessional style of humour.

Ensuing decades brought a career dip as "alternative" humour and his reputation for somewhat vulgar humour (in an age of political correctness) made him feel redundant. As he matured, Howerd's rather lugubrious physiognomy, what the comic himself referred to as his air of "a disreputable bloodhound, or a melancholy camel" may have been why Michael Parkinson – referring to Tony Hancock's sad demise – in a Seventies interview, asked if he agreed with the perception of the comedian as a lonely figure. Parkinson pushed this to query if he'd ever contemplated suicide. Howerd wryly replied, "No, but I've contemplated murder!"

An intense workaholic, Howerd's leisure time was limited, playing the odd game of tennis or meeting showbiz pals like Cilla Black, June Whitfield or Ernie Wise. The last 20 years of his life

were spent largely in Somerset with longtime partner Dennis Heymer, a sommelier he'd met in London in the late Fifties whilst dining with Sir John Mills. Heymer, ostensibly his business manager, was an invaluably calm foil for the more volatile Howerd.

When the early Nineties rolled around Howerd's reputation was again in the ascendant, embraced enthusiastically by students at the Oxford Union and elsewhere, for whom he represented the best of British humour. After 40-plus years in the profession his expressive face and indignant eyebrows, his gurgles and mock horror were all that was needed to elicit adoration.

As biographer Graham McCann asserts, his decision "to adopt such an 'ordinary' pose and persona took real wit, imagination and guts," but it stood him in good stead. While his contemporaries remained content to step back and soak up the applause, he chose to step forward and make a connection . . . That was his real achievement. His great achievement. Frankie Howerd really did make a difference."

and shows Howerd at his best, playing a fictionalised version of himself.

1969-70: Appears as the scheming Lurcio in two series of *Up Pompeii* on TV. It's a hit.

1971: Film of *Up Pompeii* released. Howerd voted 9th most popular star of the year.

1990: Last West End show at the Garrick Theatre. Appears at the Oxford Union and receives a wildly enthusiastic reception.

1992: Final series *Frankie's On . . .* appears. Still planning next ventures before he dies on 19 April of a heart attack and is buried in Somerset, his home for 20 years.

Competitors can race up to eight dogs

CALL OF THE
WILD

John Greeves speaks to Matt Hammersley about the
English husky racing scene

Dry land racing is most common in England

The Forest of Dean, a popular racing spot

Matt, ready to race

IN a chilling wintry dawn, while the rest of the country sleeps, Matt Hammersley can be found bounding through Gloucestershire's Forest of Dean with his trusty band of Siberian Huskies. This is an early morning ritual he's enjoyed for over 20 years. Matt has been captivated by husky racing since childhood, when he first read about the Iditarod Trail Sled Dog Race, which covers around 1,000 miles of Alaskan wilderness. For him, the romance of the sport lay in the experience of travelling through a frozen landscape with only dogs for company, and this continues to inspire him throughout his life.

In England today, various husky-racing events take place across the country from October to March. Most of these events consist of dry land racing (no snow required), where the drivers, or "mushers", use three-wheel all-terrain vehicles known as rigs.

Popular races include events at the Forest of Dean, Nottingham, New Forest and Thetford. The Forest of Dean event is particularly well-known, having been running for over 25 years. Races take place in the grounds of the historic Speech House hunting lodge, and 60-100 competitors take part, with around 150 spectators. It's a growing sport, with over 500 teams across the country and upwards of 70 events held annually in the UK. For Matt and his wife, Ems, the sport has taken them all over the world in their 21 years of competing. It is a sport where men and women compete as equals, and in the 2020 World Cup, Ems came second in the four-dog Nordic class and was in the top 10 in the World Championships. Matt has enjoyed considerable racing success, too, and is an International Race Marshal – the highest race judge qualification in the world, of which there are only eight representatives.

Many different breeds of sled dog take part in the racing, from Alaskan Malamutes to Siberian Huskies, American Eskimos to Chinook dogs. Matt's fixation has always been Siberian Huskies.

"I've always wanted a Siberian Husky from an early age, being an outdoor type of person," he said.

As a child, Matt asked his parents for a husky puppy every Christmas, but it would be years before he got his own dogs and eventually started a team. Matt and Ems have always bred their own huskies, requiring lengthy research to initially establish a well-proven bloodline. Over the >

> years they've built up their team, with Matt racing up to eight dogs at once. Matt's current team of canines, known as Tanglefoot, has six dogs. The sport is based on athletic performance, so the diet and fitness of the dogs is of the utmost importance. Training must be consistent and is a process for the musher as well as the dogs, as they must work together as a team. Matt ordinarily runs his huskies in pairs, and uses experienced dogs to train younger pups. Keeping them fit involves two or three sessions a week. He might use a heavy cart or a quad-bike initially, later switching to a lighter rig as he builds up the fitness and conditioning of his team and extends the distance of the runs. The dogs' training begins in autumn when the days begin to chill.

"It means getting up at three or four am, especially when it's cool, to keep the dogs fit," Matt said. "We focus on training them in regard to overtaking other dogs and being overtaken so they have good trail etiquette and are well socialised. A close bond exists, with a strong mutual trust developed on both sides," he said.

If the dogs don't trust you, Matt explains, they'll refuse to run when you need them to, or go so fast they cause you to lose control. Matt has earned both the trust and affection of his dogs, and always ensures they're cared for.

Between the early morning training sessions and the racing season, the dogs' welfare is paramount. They require constant attention and racing-sled dogs are known for being amongst the best cared for animals in the world. Competitive husky racing is governed by the International Federation of Sleddog Sports' strict rules, which ensure the dogs are healthy and well looked after.

"We are constantly looking at and checking the dogs. A process that starts before the race, during and after," Matt said. He, like other mushers, communicates with his dogs in a unique way. He uses a series of commands to direct the dogs. These include "haw" to indicate a left turn, "gee" for right,

Ems racing with her team

"gor" for straight on and "whoa" to slow down. These commands are used throughout the global husky-racing community and most owe their origins to the pack-horse drivers of the past. According to Matt, the quieter the musher is, the better the team.

"We literally speak as I am speaking now. You don't need to shout as all the dogs have excellent hearing," he explained.

British sled-dog races are generally held on looped courses through forests, with each team released at time intervals. Distances vary, with junior races spanning up to two miles, while adult classes can involve races between three and five miles. The average speed ranges between 12 to 16mph, with top speeds of 23 to 25mph, and even higher with elite teams. In dry land racing, dogs are hitched to the rig or sled by a central rope known as a gang line, with the dogs in individually fitted harnesses. Teams are divided into classes based on the number of dogs, with classes ranging from two-dog sled teams up to eight.

The sport has diverged in recent years with the inclusion of Cani-Cross, which consists of one dog and a competitor on foot, and Bike-Joring, with one dog and a driver pedalling on a bike. In the UK the most popular class of racing is currently a two-dog team, although it's not unusual to see a six or even an eight-dog rig event.

While there isn't much occasion for it in England, Matt says everyone in the sport dreams of

racing on snow. He has been lucky enough to have the opportunity to race on snow on several occasions, mostly on trips to races in Scotland and in various European countries. This calls for a state-of-the-art sledge: a Danler Hornet, made from carbon fibre and lightweight alloy, complete with skis. This gives a totally different experience from dry land racing, and Matt recalls one trip to Italy as a standout memory.

"Being on snow is magical. The dogs are silent, you don't hear any noise, just the swish of the runners as they move over the snow and the odd jingle of something on a dog's collar. In Italy there were signs of wolves and amazing scenery in the Dolomites. Another day, everywhere was covered in fresh snow, the pines blanketed with four or five inches, and I'm thinking, this is incredible and I'm here alone with my dogs," he said.

These occasions have allowed Matt to live out the snowy fantasy he pictured when he first discovered husky racing. However, snow or no snow, the biggest attraction for him remains the time he spends in the wilderness closer to home with his dogs, watching a raw sunrise in freezing temperatures and drinking in the breath-taking scenery.

"If you take it down to its purest form, it's just the simple joy of running dogs. That bond that exists between you and your dogs and teamwork in its ideal sense."
Details of upcoming husky racing events across the country can be found at snopeak.com.

Images: Fay Frost, Matt Hammersley, Shutterstock

THE CASE OF THE PILTDOWN MAN

It was 70 years ago that the famous "prehistoric" remains were shown to be a forgery. Paul Bloomfield investigates

WHEN Arthur Smith Woodward rose to address the Geological Society in London on 18 December 1912, he faced an avid audience. Joining the society's Fellows, no fewer than 74 guests had squeezed into the meeting room in Burlington Gardens, lured by a headline in the *Manchester Guardian*: "The Earliest Man? Remarkable Discovery in Sussex". They weren't disappointed.

"The skull may be regarded as presenting a hitherto unknown species of *Homo*," Woodward, keeper of geology at what is now the Natural History Museum, declared. The remains presented were, he said, fossil evidence of *Eoanthropus dawsoni* – "Dawson's dawn man", named for his co-speaker that night, amateur archaeologist Charles Dawson.

Today, the "species" is better known as Piltdown Man, from the Sussex village where the men had unearthed these relics. It's also known as one of the greatest hoaxes in the history of science.

Woodward's excitement – and, with hindsight, credulity – is easy to understand. Over previous decades, a string of paleontological discoveries in France, Germany and Indonesia had rewritten the prehistory books, revolutionising understanding of human evolution. No wonder Woodward, alerted to Dawson's initial finds in a letter of February 1912, was so keen to believe the Piltdown remains represented a new pre-human species – and a British one at that. Over the following months, the men turned up more objects in Sussex. Dark-brown fragments of

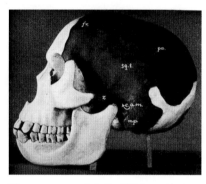

The reconstructed skull of Piltdown Man

a human-like cranium, a mandible with simian characteristics and a couple of worn teeth, were augmented by animal fossils and flint tools. Could this be the longed-for "missing link"?

"Although not everyone agreed, even at the time of publication, many experts hailed the Piltdown discoveries as representing the clearest example of an evolutionary transition between apes and humans," Professor Chris Stringer, an expert in human evolution at the Natural History Museum, explains.

Most British scientists, hungry to accept these conclusions, ignored any doubts for decades. It wasn't until 1949 that fluorine tests conducted by a Natural History Museum geologist showed the remains were much younger than claimed. Further analysis revealed that the skull fragments were human, the jaw probably from an orangutan; the molars had been filed to resemble human teeth, and all had been stained to appear much older. The game was up

and in 1953 Piltdown Man was declared a hoax.

"The exposure showed that many scientists had been deceived and diverted from properly assessing other, genuine fossils of ancient human relatives," Stringer says. "But it also made others more vigilant, and showed that the scientific process could expose such forgeries and validate the fossil record."

More recent studies suggest that only one hoaxer was likely responsible. "Our research showed that Charles Dawson was centrally involved in the forgery, with the probable motive of scientific fame and status," Stringer explains.

Today, those deceptive bones and teeth are stored among the wonders of the Natural History Museum in London, where they are sometimes displayed. Visitors to Piltdown will unearth no ancient remains, merely a few houses along quiet Sussex backroads. There's a pub renamed The Piltdown Man, and a stone memorial within the private grounds of Barkham Manor – the only reminders of a discovery that fooled Britain's scientific establishment and fleetingly upturned ideas of human evolution.

Excavations at Piltdown

Christmas tree and wreath at 10 Downing Street

DECK THE HALLS

Holly, ivy, mistletoe – Christmas wouldn't be the same without traditional festive greenery, says Hazel Reynolds

Christmas trees for sale at a nursery in Wimbledon

Bright red berries on a holly branch

Victorian greeting card showing a family decorating for Christmas

Children help the Duchess of Cornwall decorate the tree at Clarence House

Deck the halls with boughs of holly
Fa-la-la-la-la, la-la-la-la
'Tis the season to be jolly
Fa-la-la-la-la, la-la-la-la.
Thomas Oliphant (1799–1873)

WE all love to decorate our homes at Christmas. In fact, retailers bombard us with an astonishing array of Christmas decorations and trees from the end of August. Last year I recall seeing a Christmas tree in a neighbour's home in September!

With trees and decorations being put up earlier every year, the emphasis is often on elaborate ornaments and "bling", not to mention the brilliance and sparkle of exterior Christmas light displays in gardens across the country. However, we still aspire to the ideal image of a sitting room with a glowing log fire, garlands of fresh holly and ivy and the smell of fresh pine needles from the bedecked real tree in the corner.

As with so many of our traditions, the use of greenery at

Decking the halls circa 1880

this time of the year has its origins in pagan times. Druids celebrated the Winter Solstice on the shortest day of the year, 21 December, with holly, ivy and mistletoe. Evergreen plants were believed to represent new life and give hope for spring.

The ancient Druids hung mistletoe to bring good luck and to ward off evil spirits. They are also thought to have begun the tradition of burning a yule log; once again, to banish evil. The origin of

kissing under the mistletoe comes from Norse mythology, where it was used as a sign of love and friendship. Interestingly, the name mistletoe comes from two Anglo-Saxon words: "Mistel" which means dung and "tan", meaning twig or stick. The literal translation doesn't really have a ring to it!

The first Christians, arriving from Western Europe, tried to ban the use of mistletoe as a decoration in churches, but many continued. York Minster is still the only cathedral in England which places both mistletoe and ivy on its high altar at Christmas. The Minster used to hold a winter mistletoe service where York's wrongdoers were invited to be pardoned.

Holding up a branch of mistletoe, the priest would declare, "public and universal liberty, pardon and freedom of all sorts of inferior and wicked people at the minster gates, and the gates of the city, towards the four quarters of heaven." Although the service is no longer offered, the sprig of mistletoe on the altar is a reminder of forgiveness.

Some pagans believed that holly >

Decorating the tree at Brodsworth Hall, Yorkshire

> was a male plant and ivy a female plant. One Midlands tradition stated that whichever of the plants was brought into the house first during the winter, signified whether the man or the woman would rule the household during that year! It was thought unlucky, however, to bring either plant indoors before Christmas Eve.

Christians placed different interpretations on the plants. The prickly leaves of holly represent the crown of thorns worn by Jesus when he was crucified, the berries being the drops of his blood.

The holly and the ivy,
When they are both full grown,
Of all the trees that are in the
*   wood,*
The holly bears the crown.

The holly bears a berry
As red as any blood
And Mary bore sweet Jesus Christ
For to do us sinners good.

The holly bears a prickle,
As sharp as any thorn,
And Mary bore sweet Jesus Christ
On Christmas Day in the morn.
Sharp's English Folk Carols
(1911)

As ivy clings to support itself, we are reminded that we should cling to God for support. The laurel wreath represents victory and is said to symbolise the victory of God over the Devil. Evergreen yew and fir trees signify everlasting life with God.

Rosemary, for remembrance and friendship, is often used in wreaths and garlands. It was a common garnish in the Middle Ages, placed on a boar's head as people enjoyed their Christmas meal. It also acts as a reminder of the birth of Jesus.

The hanging of a circular wreath is thought to date back to the Romans, when they were hung on doors as a sign of victory or status. Rich Roman women wore them as a headdress and Roman emperors are depicted wearing laurel wreaths. The word "wreath" comes from the Old English "writhen", meaning to coil or twist.

Kissing boughs or balls, dating back to the Middle Ages, may have originated from wreaths. Made from five hoops of foliage, four of which were vertical with the fifth made to go around the middle to form the ball, they were covered with holly, ivy, rosemary, bay and fir. Hung from a colourful ribbon, a centre of fruit or an image of Christ was often placed inside the ball. Some households would crown the bough with candles, before adding the final touch of the all-important bunch of mistletoe.

Before the introduction of Christmas trees, the kissing bough was often the centre of the home during the festive period. Boughs were particularly popular in Tudor times, and then the Victorians hung them from doorways, chandeliers and ceilings at Christmas.

The poinsettia plant, native to Central America, was known by the Aztecs as "Cuetlaxochitl" and was widely used to make dyes and for medicines. Their popularity at Christmas is credited to Joel Roberts Poinsett, appointed first US Ambassador to Mexico in 1825. He cultivated the plants in greenhouses, sending them to friends and botanical gardens. The shape of the plant is thought to resemble the Star of Bethlehem, the red leaves symbolising the blood of Christ and the white leaves representing his purity.

It was during the Victorian Era when the main greenery of Christmas was introduced into many homes. The Christmas tree!

O Christmas Tree,
O Christmas Tree,
How steadfast are your branches!
Your boughs are green in
*   summer's clime*
And through the snows of
*   wintertime.*
O Christmas Tree,
O Christmas Tree,
How steadfast are your branches!
From the German O

Rows of poinsettias at Hills Plants, West Sussex

Harvesting mistletoe in South Gloucestershire

Tannenbaum, Modern lyrics by Ernst Anschütz.

Firs were first used as Christmas trees in Northern Europe, and may have been hung upside down from chains attached to the ceiling! Other plants were put in pots and brought indoors to flower at Christmas or, if a real plant was too expensive, wooden pyramid trees were constructed and decorated with paper, apples and candles. These may have imitated Paradise Trees, used in German mystery plays on Christmas Eve, and thought to represent the Garden of Eden.

The first documented public Christmas tree is disputed between the cities of Tallinn in Estonia and Riga in Latvia. They claim they erected the trees in their town squares: Tallinn in 1441 and Riga in 1510. It's possible this custom travelled from Latvia to Germany.

Many of the well-known legends and sightings of Christmas trees originate in Germany. The 16th-century German preacher, Martin Luther, is thought to be the first person to add lighted candles on to an indoor Christmas tree. Aside from candles, the first Christmas trees were decorated with edible items including gingerbread and apples, before glass ornaments were produced.

Germany was, and still is, famed for producing tree ornaments. Having lived in Germany as a child while my father served in the RAF, I recall returning to England with large commercial biscuit tins full of beautifully crafted German tree ornaments. I still have some of them today, over 60 years later.

Although Prince Albert is credited with introducing the Christmas tree into the mainstream in Victorian Britain, Queen Charlotte, wife of George III, first displayed a Christmas tree at Windsor Castle for a children's party in 1800. The young Princess Victoria also had a tree placed in her room for Christmas 1832, recording it in her journal.

Prince Albert imported German firs into Britain in 1840 to be displayed in Windsor Castle. The trees were mainly decorated with candles, which would pose health and safety issues today and probably require a detailed risk assessment! The popularity of decorated Christmas trees quickly spread as adverts for trees appeared in newspapers. An illustrated book, *The Christmas Tree*, describing their history and use, was published in December 1844. Newspapers delighted in describing the royal Christmas trees in detail, accompanied by illustrations of the happy family. Up until the 1920s, it was mainly the wealthy who could afford trees, but eventually everyone was able to enjoy celebrating Christmas with decorated trees.

Although there are a range of artificial trees available in various colours and shapes, the real tree is still a first choice and "choosing the tree" is, for many, a family tradition. Trees are grown all over the UK with the Norway Spruce being the most popular for many years. Now, however, there is demand for the non-drop Nordmann Fir. The choice of lights and decorations is mind-boggling, with dedicated Christmas shops open all year and special areas in department stores offering an amazing choice. I've visited specialist Christmas shops in Berlin and Bruges, stocking dazzling and expensive displays.

It's hard to imagine Christmas without greenery and trees. Traditional crafts are making a comeback so why not explore the hedgerows and countryside for holly, ivy and mistletoe, and deck the halls this Christmas?

GUESS THE STATELY HOME
AT CHRISTMAS

We have some magnificent Christmas interiors for you to guess, with some suitable clues…

Answers on p107

1. This royal castle always puts on a good display in its **St George's Hall** – where is it?

2. The **Great Dining Room** of this famous house, which is often described as the jewel in the crown of the Peak District. What is it?

3. Home to the Rothschilds, this Buckinghamshire mansion always puts on a good winter light display. What is it?

4. One of our most famous PMs was born here. In which house is this understated (!) dining room?

NTI/Chris Johnson

5. This Cheshire mansion is famous for its RHS Flower Show in the grounds. What is it?

NTI/Megan Taylor

6. This National Trust house was designed by Philip Webb and features many William Morris fabrics. What is it?

7 A Tudor and Jacobean gem in Lancashire that was home to the Hesketh Family for 500 years. Name that hall . . .

11. This festive cottage in Somerset was briefly home to one of our leading romantic poets and is named after him. What is it called?

8. This is the library of Queen Victoria's favourite Prime Minister and the house played a crucial role in World War II. What is it?

12. This spectacular Jacobean Norfolk hall is on the site of a manor thought to have been the birthplace of Anne Boleyn. What is it?

9. This Cornish National Trust house boasts a remarkable flower garland every Christmas. What is the name of the house?

13. This Cornish house sits above the River Fowey, is in the care of the National Trust and is known for its gardens. What is it?

10. This Berkshire mansion, which appeared in *Pride and Prejudice* (2005) was a **POW** camp, then rescued by the Iliffe family. What is it?

14. Skate in style outside this magnificent royal palace on the banks of the Thames, one time home to Henry VIII. What is it?

Images: Shutterstock, Alamy and Chatsworth; National Trust Images (NTI)

THEY CHANGED OUR WORLD

Tallulah Rushaya on the rise of the supermarket

Co-op shopper

THE daily routine for millions of us involves going to the supermarket. While it's a simple task that we probably take for granted, it has revolutionised how we shop. From branded shopping bags to slogans and specific favourites found only in particular shops, supermarkets identify us as much as our clothes.

It wasn't always thus. Britain's supermarket history is rooted in a gradual evolution from humble grocer to these retail giants – and from hypermarkets back down again to the express store, the new face of the traditional corner shop. According to author and food historian Emma Kay, the first reference she found to the word supermarket "is in 1921, as a phrase used to describe Southampton, which was becoming a bit of a retail magnet for surrounding rural dwellers at this time." The supermarket, as we have come to know it though, stems from America, where the world's oldest is believed to be Piggly Wiggly, which opened in 1916, Memphis, Tennessee. It provided a template for some British entrepreneurs, who would go on to transform the shopping experience. In Britain, there were several attempts to open self-service stores, including one from as early as "1927 in Hammersmith, London called Value Ltd, advertising their new system of shopping without shopping," Emma says.

It wasn't until 32 years after Piggly Wiggly's launch, on 12 January 1948, that a branch of the London Co-operative Society opened. It would later be the Co-op, but this was the first recognised self-service supermarket. It opened in Manor Park in East Ham, Essex (now the London Borough of Newham). In a time of austerity, the idea of being able to buy products for less than the price paid previously was viewed as a welcome relief for some, with the additional benefit of job opportunities.

"These new stores also increased employment with more than half a million retailers recruiting one British worker in eight to serve in a shop in 1955," Emma explains.

However, despite the novelty and curiosity, some were confused by the idea of lifting items from a shelf. The hesitation came from potential prosecution for touching items in grocery shops. While others did not find queuing appealing, especially if only purchasing one or two items.

When Marks & Spencer conducted their own self-service trial just prior to Co-op's launch in 1947, they noted that many of their colleagues disliked being on cashier duty, missing "having their own counter". But they also noted, interestingly, that food department sales rose significantly during the trial. *The Grocer*, the leading trade magazine for food retailers, summed up the scepticism by writing in 1947, "The people of this country have long been accustomed to counter-service, and it is doubtful whether they would be content to wander round a store hunting for goods." Despite the apprehension, Tesco, Marks & Spencer, Sainsbury's, and Waitrose soon followed suit with self-service. After a slow start and once rationing had ended, there was rapid growth in the 1950s and 1960s. Emma says, "Self-service stores replacing conventional stores was happening at a rate of two every day in 1958."

Prior to supermarkets, grocers were often family-run stores that sold freshly grown produce. "Grocery stores have been on the streets of England since the 1600s. They sold a combination of staple commodities and luxury imported goods, such as coffee, chocolate, tea, sugar, and spices. The Company of Grossers, which eventually morphed into Grocers, was founded in London as early as 1373," Emma explains. "These were shops that catered to both the wealthy and the poor in different ways. While the privileged benefited from products on credit, the labouring classes were served out of a window, typically on a cash purchase basis."

Customers would provide a list of what they required, with a shop

Wood Green self service food department Marks & Spencer, 1948

Tesco in the Victoria Centre, 1985

Waite, Rose and Taylor, first branch in 1906

The Co-op in Ellesmere Port

Tesco – a new store opens

Notice from M&S

A Tesco store assistant restocking

Counter display at the Co-op

J. Sainsbury's advertising artwork 1930s

Interior of Ashford High Street Sainsbury's 1961

Tesco store interior

assistant ready to retrieve items from shelves and measure products such as flour. With the grocers, there were butchers, bakeries, and fishmongers where service was also personalised. While this meant going to multiple shops in a day, the shopping experience was more elaborate and hospitable. With such assistance, it's no wonder that the introduction of self-service came as a shock to shoppers.

Although some grocers adapted to the change, others were more reluctant, and some found they were too small to convert to self-service which led to some grocers shutting up shop. The new way to shop came with challenges in creating strategic displays to entice shoppers with brand names, >

> particularly with everything under one roof. Founder of Tesco, Jack Cohen, coined the phrase "Pile it high and sell it cheap". Despite lower prices, it took a while for shoppers to become accustomed to the changes. In 1950, at a Sainsbury's in Croydon, it is said one frustrated shopper threw their basket at Alan Sainsbury, who had implemented the idea of self-service and was also the grandson of founder John James Sainsbury.

The economic boom of the '60s led to more car owners and larger retail spaces and the start of out of town sites. Transport was not the only thing that changed. The rising popularity of the electric freezer led to increased numbers buying frozen food in the 1960s and '70s. Along came another recognisable UK supermarket, aptly named Iceland, founded in 1970 in Oswestry, Shropshire, by Malcolm Walker and business partner Peter Hinchcliffe. In the 1970s and 1980s Artic rolls, Black Forest gateaux, peas and fish fingers were commonplace in our freezers.

While Iceland took off in the 1980s, another was on the horizon. Aldi, a German supermarket, came to UK shores on 5 April 1990 without a single advertisement, opening its first store in Stechford, Birmingham. Aldi's roots stretch back to 1913, to a humble suburb of Essen, Germany. Theo and Karl Albrecht took over their mother's business, opening "the first discount store in the world". Aldi has stuck to a pattern of a small product range, store size and staff numbers. Subsequently, Lidl, another German export, opened in the UK in 1994. It was founded by Dieter Schwarz in 1977, the son of a general food wholesaler. Dieter's father was the partner of a company that had the "Lidl" name in its title. Starting originally with ten stores in the UK, in the space of three years it had opened distribution centres and had welcomed one million customers by 2003. Despite past false rumours of Aldi and Lidl either being an anagram for one another or the same store, it is undeniable

A BRIEF HISTORY OF SUPERMARKETS

- **1869** John James Sainsbury and his wife Mary Ann established their first shop in Holborn, London. They were pioneers in own-brand goods.
- **1882** Sainsbury's opened its first branch outside London at 6 London Road, Croydon.
- **1884** Michael Marks opened a Penny Bazaar in Leeds. In 1894 Michael went into business with Tom Spencer who developed what we know as Marks & Spencer.
- **1899** William Morrison, an egg and butter merchant, opened a stall in Bradford Market. In 1952, his son Sir Ken Morrison took over the small group market stalls.
- **1904** Waite, Rose & Taylor began life on Acton High Street, founded by Wallace Wyndham Waite, Arthur Rose and David Taylor. Taylor left in 1908 and the remaining duo formed Waitrose.
- **1919** Jack Cohen sold surplus groceries from a stall in Hackney in London's East End. His first Tesco store was opened in 1929 in Burnt Oak, Edgware in Middlesex.
- **1937** Wallace Waite met Michael Watkins, Director of Trading for John Lewis. In October 1937, ten Waitrose shops and 160 staff joined the John Lewis Partnership.
- **24 November 1947** M&S trialled self-service food halls.
- **12 January 1948** The London Co-Operative Society opened in Manor Park, East London.
- **1948** Tesco opened their first supermarket in Maldon, Essex.
- **26 June 1950** Sainsbury's opened their first self-service food store on London Road, Croydon.
- **1955** Sainsbury's opens the largest self-service food store in Europe, in Lewisham, adding bread and fresh produce for the first time.
- **1958** The first town-centre Morrisons opens with three checkouts, the only self-service store in Bradford and the only one to have prices on its products.
- **1970** Iceland opened its first shop in autumn in Oswestry, Shropshire.
- **1972** M&S introduced "sell by" dates which later became a legal requirement for other supermarkets.
- **1990** Aldi opened their first UK store in Stechford, Birmingham.
- **1994** Lidl opened their first 10 stores across the UK.
- **2000** Ocado.com is launched online only going into partnership with Waitrose in 2002.
- **2005** Most leading supermarkets offer self-service tills.
- **2021** Amazon Fresh opens its first till-free convenience store in Ealing, London.

that British shopping was changed in the 1990s with these discounters. Initially the two stores were not acclaimed as they are today, due to the British being less price conscious compared to Germans. Their popularity has been a recent surprise.

The supermarket is always adapting to consumers. By 1998 they had started testing or offering home delivery. When self-service checkouts were introduced in 2003, starting in Tesco, and gradually rolled out elsewhere, reactions were again divided. Some shoppers echoed concerns

that self-checkout would add to diminishing social interactions. However, now, it would be difficult to imagine shops without them.

After online retailer Amazon opened their first cashierless shop in March 2021, Tesco followed suit. In October 2021, the chain became the first major UK supermarket to open a checkoutless shop in Holborn, using technology that is linked to a customer's account. In 75 years, the supermarket has become more than simply a place to shop and it will be interesting to see how it continues to evolve.

QUIZ ANSWERS

BROUGHT TO BOOK FROM PAGE 25

1. *The Hobbit*
2. Beat author Jack Kerouac
3. 1956
4. David Suchet
5. *Nineteen Eighty-Four*
6. 120 million
7. Whitby, where author Bram Stoker holidayed and where he set the start of the novel

8. North London
9. Gentleman farmer George Knightley
10. William Brown in Richmal Crompton's *Just William*
11. *The Thursday Murder Club* by *Pointless* TV star Richard Osman, in 2020
12. 700
13. *The Hitchhiker's Guide to the Galaxy*, by Douglas Adams (as spoken by computer Deep Thought)
14. Lucky Jim, published 1954
15. G.K. Chesterton, creator of priest-detective Father Brown
16. Shakespeare's *The Winter's Tale*
17. W. Somerset Maugham
18. Eric Sykes
19. *Carrie* (1973)
20. 1926, in the book simply called *Winnie-the-Pooh*

THE TOUGH *THIS ENGLAND* POLITICS QUIZ FROM PAGE 74

Gossip and Scandal
1. David Warburton
2. David Mellor
3. Back to Basics
4. Jeremy Thorpe
5. A floating duck house, costing about £1,600
6. John Stonehouse
7. Sasha Swire
8. Ken Livingstone
9. Matt Hancock and Gina Coladangelo
10. John Prescott

Dates, Stats and History
11. Sir Robert Walpole
12. Six: Ramsay MacDonald, Clement Attlee, Harold Wilson, Jim Callaghan, Tony Blair and Gordon Brown
13. David Lloyd George, who served between 1916 and 1922
14. 14
15. James Callaghan
16. Sir Robert Walpole, 20 years, 314 days; William Pitt the Younger, 18 years, 343 days; Robert Jenkinson, Earl of Liverpool, 14 years, 305 days
17. 1950 and 1951
18. 1975
19. 28
20. William Gladstone

Behind the Power
21. Geoffrey Howe
22. Nadine Dorries
23. Neville Chamberlain, Clement Attlee, Viscount Halifax, Arthur Greenwood and Winston Churchill
24. Denis Healey
25. Benjamin Disraeli
26. Michael Portillo
27. Anthony Eden
28. Mo Mowlam
29. Amber Rudd
30. Michael Heseltine and Leon Brittan

True or False
31. True
32. False – it was Harold Macmillan's
33. True
34. False – it appeared in 1978
35. False – it was David Cameron, though it's not exactly what he said
36. True
37. True
38. False – it was at the restaurant Granita in Islington
39. False – it was his many infidelities
40. False – she claimed to "love him like a father"

GUESS THE STATELY HOME AT CHRISTMAS FROM PAGE 102

1. Windsor Castle
2. Chatsworth House
3. Waddesdon Manor
4. Blenheim Palace
5. Tatton Park
6. Standen House and Garden
7. Rufford Old Hall
8. Hughenden Manor
9. Cotehele
10. Basildon Park
11. Coleridge Cottage
12. Blickling Hall
13. Lanhydrock
14. Hampton Court Palace

The quarterly issues of This England are every bit as enjoyable as this annual edition; in fact even more so! Each quarterly issue of This England magazine celebrates England's countryside, customs, history and heritage accompanied by beautiful seasonal photographs. It also has a lively letters page, with readers exchanging views and sharing memories on all sorts of subjects.

This England is cherished by readers far and wide but it's not always easy to get hold of a copy in the shops. With a subscription you can be sure to receive each seasonal issue. Subscribe today and get your first issue for only £1, that's just £16 for the whole year, with free UK delivery direct to your door. When you take out a direct debit or 2 year pre-paid subscription you'll also receive one of our stunning Country Calendars absolutely FREE, worth £7.99.

Angela Linforth, Editor

GREAT REASONS TO SUBSCRIBE...

- **SAVE OVER 80%** on the shop price via Direct Debit — only £16 for one year.

- **FREE** greetings card available, on request, with each gift subscription.

- **FREE** This England Country Calendar when you pay by direct debit or take out a 2 or 3 year pre-paid subscription, worth £7.99.

- **FREE** UK delivery, direct to your door.

- **GUARANTEED** lowest price direct from the publisher.

- **NEVER MISS** an issue.

THIS ENGLAND
Country Calendar 2023

FREE CALENDAR

BEST DEAL		
DIRECT DEBIT	**1 YEAR PREPAY**	**2 YEAR PREPAY**
ONLY £16.00 First issue £1 then £5 per quarter thereafter.	£22.00 £19.80	£41.80 £37.62
SAVE 82% +FREE calendar	SAVE 10%	SAVE 10% +FREE calendar

'I look forward to every issue of your magazine, I subscribe to several British publications but none can compare to This England.'
J F MCGUCKIN.

'A fantastic read. It is one of the few magazines you can pick up and read again and again.'
L LAVELLE.

IT'S EASY TO SUBSCRIBE:

📱 CALL: **0800 074 0188** Quoting code: **ANN23**

(Free from UK landlines and mobiles) Mon-Fri 8am-6pm. Overseas: +44 1382 575052

THIS ENGLAND
FANTASTIC SUBSCRIPTION OFFER
Save over 80% on your first issue

FIRST ISSUE ONLY £1*

VISIT: **www.thisengland.co.uk/ann23**